D1827382

About this Book

Lean Production for the Office--Common Sense Ideas to Help Your Office Continuously Improve is for anyone who works in an office and seeks practical information on how to make your continuous improvement program a huge success.

Stop obsessing about benchmarking, and use your own and your team's creativity and ingenuity to leap-frog over your competition. Then let them benchmark you!

Lean Production for the Office teaches you how to make your office smarter – by focusing on the value-added elements while eliminating waste, and by replacing frustration with happiness.

Author, Jim Thompson, proves that lean production need not be intimidating. **Lean Production for the Office** is easy to read and provides a few laughs as well.

About the Author

Jim Thompson studied lean production first hand as a member of the GM Technical Liaison Office with NUMMI (a GM/Toyota joint venture) in Fremont, California. It was there that he and his teammates began applying lean production techniques to the office environment.

He is now President of In*Sight Management, Inc, a lean production teaching and consulting firm located in Rochester, Michigan. He has also published three other books on lean production: *The Lean Office--How to use Just-in-Time Techniques to Streamline Your Office, Lean Production–How to Use the Highly Effective Japanese Concept of Kaizen to Improve Your Efficiency* and *The Old Mission Academy–A Novel of One Charter School's Experiences Implementing Lean Education.*

He holds a B.A., M.A., Ed.S. and M.B.A. from the University of Michigan.

· LEAN PRODUCTION ·
· FOR THE OFFICE ·

COMMON SENSE IDEAS
TO HELP YOUR OFFICE
CONTINUOUSLY IMPROVE

JIM THOMPSON

ISBN: 1-55270-025-9

Written by:
Jim Thompson

Mr. Thompson is available as a consultant in **Just-in-Time Techniques** and can be contacted <u>in writing</u> care of the publisher, at the address given below.

Published in Canada by:
Productive Publications, P.O. Box 7200,
Station A, Toronto, Ont. M5W 1X8
Phone: (416) 483-0634
Fax: (416) 322-7434

Copyright © 2000 by Jim Thompson

National Library of Canada cataloging

Thompson, Jim, 1945-
    Lean production for the office : common sense
ideas to help your office continuously improve

ISBN 1-55270-025-9

    1. Management. I. Title

HF5547.T536 2000   658.4   C00-900689-3

HOW TO ORDER

ONLINE

USA: *www.LeanTeamBooks.biz*

Canada: *www.LeanTeamBooks.ca*

UK: *www.ameritech.co.uk*

PHONE, FAX or MAIL

USA & CANADA:

Productive Publications
1939 Yonge St., # 1210, Toronto, Ontario M4S 1Z4
Canada
Phone: (416) 483-0634 Fax: (416) 322-7434
Toll-Free Order Line: 1-(877) 879-2669
Serving Readers for Over 18 years

UNITED KINGDOM:

American Technical Publishers Ltd.
27-29 Knowl Piece, Wilbury Way
Hitchin, Hertfordshire, SG4 0SX
England
Phone: +44 (0)1462 437933
Fax: +44 (0)1462 433678

Acknowledgements

I would like to thank all those who have shared with me their fascination and respect for lean production, particularly my NUMMI teammates.

I would also like to again thank Doug Jennings, of the GM Technical Liaison Office - a great friend and constant source of inspiration and support.

Acknowledgement is also given to The Corel Corporation of Ottawa, Ontario for the extensive use of their "Corel Gallery" clipart in this publication. Thanks are also due to EyeWire, Inc., of Calgary, Alberta for the use of their Image Club™ clipart drawings featured on pages 11, 40, 71, 76, 77, 83, 86,107, 128 and 136.

Dedication

To Connie, who as wife, mother, teacher, and friend demonstrates everyday that perfection is really attainable.

Table of Contents

Table of Contents

INTRODUCTION

This book, the sequel to *The Lean Office* published in 1997, is a compendium of what this author has learned through teaching, writing, observing, and listening to those pioneers implementing lean production in the office environment.

For those already applying lean production in their manufacturing activities, it is just a matter of time before lean migrates into your office activities. There is just too much opportunity for continuous improvement to pass it up.

For offices not affiliated with manufacturing, the change will come more slowly – but seems inevitable, given lean production's growth and popularity.

I have been guided and haunted by a standard for teaching I learned when working for General Motors and assigned to NUMMI, their joint venture with Toyota, in Fremont, California.

"If the student didn't learn, the teacher didn't teach."

Such a standard makes it incumbent upon the teacher to *inspect* to see whether what was being taught successfully made it from the mind of the teacher to that of the student.

After all, "You get what you *inspect*, not what you expect."

Such inspection of my own teaching as well as that of others led me to five general conclusions:

1. The common thread of lean production is the existence, detection, and ultimate elimination of waste. Yet, there is a tendency to wander from this basic premise. Those who keep focused will be well rewarded by the benefits of continuous improvement.

2. Ideas, kaizens, continuous improvement initiatives, suggestions – whatever you choose to call them are the life blood of the lean office. Managers have the power to create the environment which ultimately encourages or stifles them. To keep the spigot turned on and the ideas flowing is the role and responsibility of the leader.

3. In teaching lean production for the office, I soon came to the conclusion that *If they don't understand the concept, stop the process!* Once again, the power that can be gained by "inspecting" the learners – and by asking them *why they are*

2

doing what they are doing can reveal much – particularly where the teaching can be improved. And that is good.

4. Many seek the *effects* of this system - we love results. But just due should also be paid to its *affects*. Lean Production does amazing things to and for employees. This alone is a strong argument for practicing it.

5. Finally, the system's relentless pursuit of perfection: rather than an exercise in frustration, it is both noble and refreshing in a world where standards often seem to be going down instead of up.

Thus, the purpose of this book is to share with the reader what my friends, colleagues, and students have taught me.

I respect and admire lean production because:

●   It is environmentally friendly. It minimizes the use of resources by not making more than is needed.

●   It provides employees with the tools they need to truly "add value" and hence be vital and valuable in their jobs.

●   It treats employees like adults.

- It is imbued with possibility and hope. It expects things to continuously get better.

That's why I continue to be fascinated by it, and look forward each day to learning something new about it.

If I have properly done my job, this book will convey to the reader these concepts – which result in helping to create a culture where employees can experience the joy of being able to make a difference while at the same time helping their organization to achieve success.

Please inspect.

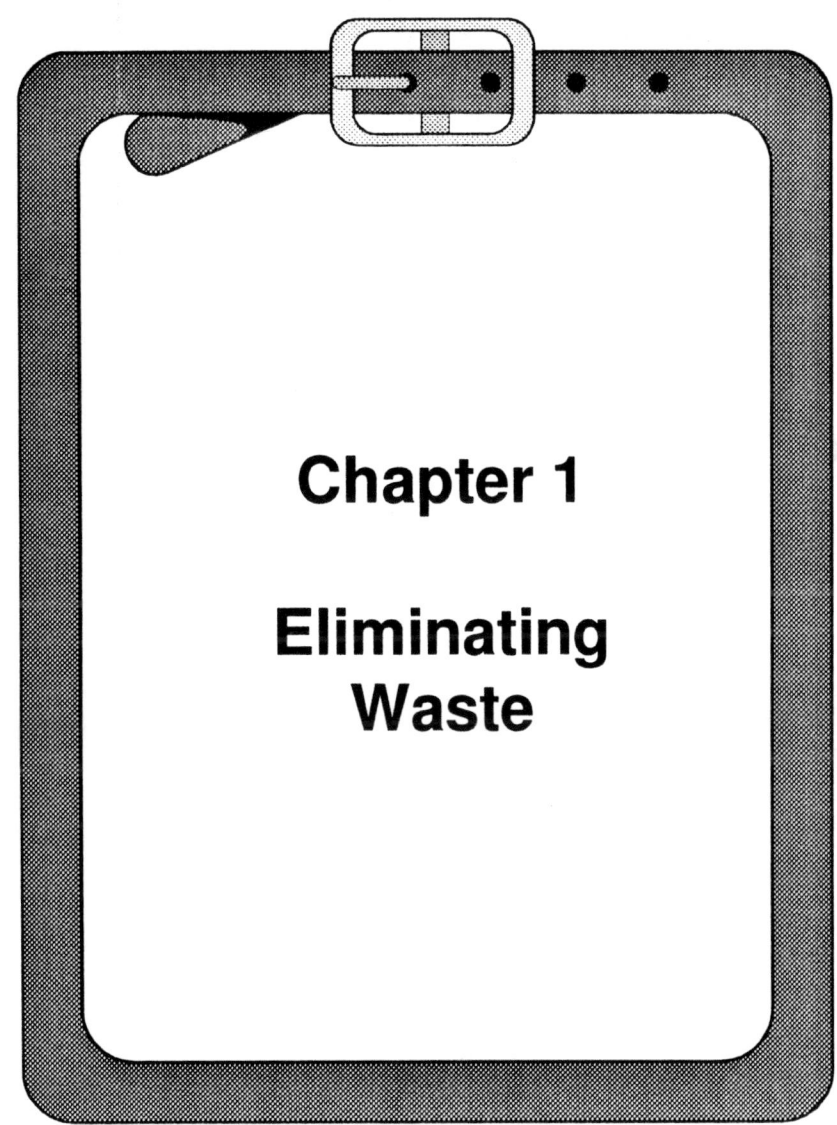

Chapter 1

Eliminating Waste

The Beginning

A small boy explains to the family pastor that the Bible is really a book about baseball.

"How can that be?" asks the incredulous clergyman.

"Easy," replies the lad. "It starts, *In the big inning...*"

Where to *begin* the discussion of lean production in the office is an important decision. There are many attractive, competing alternatives which vie for the honor.

One could argue that because the system is so inter-connected, it is but a circular path, which if followed, will eventually bring us past every base in due time.

However, logically, there is a best place to begin which makes it less likely that we might miss some "big innings" later in the game.

To find this starting point, we merely need to ask the question:

What is Purpose?

If I had to choose the most important concept I learned on my two year assignment to NUMMI, the GM and Toyota joint venture in Fremont, California, it would be to ask more questions.

Specifically, the question: "What is purpose?"

When confused by complications or competing ideas, going back to the reason "why" or the purpose for our draining the swamp in the first place often sheds light on the best path to follow.

In other words, when we know what we are *there for*, the *therefores* become clearer.

The goal or purpose of lean production as established by its chief architect, Taiichi Ohno is this:

> "The goal of The Toyota Production System is to maximize profits by lowering cost through the ***total elimination of waste***."

How we are to accomplish this goal of maximizing profits by lowering costs couldn't be more specific–by trying to completely eliminate waste.

What naturally follows, then, is that the first step to reach this goal is to learn all we can about **waste**:

1. What is it?

2. How does one detect it?

3. Then, how does one eliminate it?

Shigeo Shingo, a disciple of Ohno's, thought that the popular slogan, *Eliminate Waste* was ridiculous, as anybody who *found* waste would instinctively know it should be eliminated. The challenge, he thought, was to *detect* waste in the first place.

But to detect waste, we first need to know what it is.

This is the beginning of lean production.

The Seven Types of Waste

Other books have defined and described the seven types of waste, so we will not go into that here. (See appendix.)

This book will focus on Toyota's original seven types of waste:

- Processing
- Waiting
- Conveyance
- Overproduction
- Motion
- Inventory
- Correction

- **7 Types of Waste.**

- **7 deadly sins.**

Coincidence?

For those who can't live without acronyms, mine is <u>P</u>retty, <u>W</u>itty, <u>**COMIC**</u>.

9

Most likely, your company will use a different set of types of waste than these. Some companies, such as Boeing, use ten types of waste. Others modify the list slightly with the additions of "the waste of talent", "the waste of time", "the waste of energy", etc.

It's worth little effort to debate who has the best list. More important to the organization's success is how well they recognize and eliminate the wastes they choose to list.

The worst case is not to use a list at all.

Nothing made seven the sacred number. Adding to or deleting from the list can add a personal touch–and quite frankly–distance the company from merely copying Toyota.

But additions generally make the list harder to remember– unless the addition contributes to creating an acronym that simply can't be forgotten.

One aspect of lean production which makes it so "user friendly" is that it requires few things to be memorized. However, the list of types of waste is the foremost, because it is the chief tool with which to accomplish your mission. Creating a list that is difficult to remember is like tying your feet together before running a marathon. The issue is not whether you will finish. The issue is whether or not you can even start.

Ironically, adding more types of waste can be contributing to "the waste of inventory".

A good rule of thumb is--any additional types of waste should simply add more value than their inclusion creates confusion.

The number of types of waste should not be determined on the basis that every member of a committee gets their favorite waste included on the list!

If such is the case, pray the committee is a small one.

Deletions from the list may make the list easier to remember, but may strip it of content. Remember, Toyota has been perfecting this system for nearly half a century.

Beware of anyone trying to discard "the waste of overproduction". It is absolutely the worst, or ***most wasteful*** of the wastes--and without it, a lean system rests on a very shaky foundation.

Survival of the Fittest

Waste permeates and infects all activity. It is not always visible, and even when so, is often inconspicuous. It is therefore important for us to employ techniques and devices to expose it.

Waste generally won't kill us. But by insidiously adding more work and effort to our lives without producing any added benefit in return, it can wear us down. It serves to frustrate and discourage us and keep us from accomplishing our goals.

How well we detect and eliminate it speaks to our individual, team, and organizational wellness.

Even when detected, its symptoms are more often addressed than its root cause. For instance, my post office's cure for customer frustration with waiting in long lines was to install a TV set, anesthetizing them with CNN sights and sounds of the world's daily disasters.

Those organizations that best address their waste have the best chance of survival. Although waste probably won't kill you, it can weaken you enough so that a competitor can.

12

By using lean systems such as waste detection and elimination, continuous improvement (kaizen), the Five S, and standardized work, we can create a climate and culture that is healthier for individuals, both physically and mentally--and one that is unhealthy for waste. And this applies both to our workplaces and to our homes.

Given downsizing, rightsizing, re-engineering, merging, consolidating, and all their ilk, it is hard not to picture and describe the business world in Darwinian terms.

Survival still goes to the fittest.

Don't let waste weaken you.

Misery Loves Company

Where one type of waste is detected, other types will be lurking nearby. They travel in groups. Be leery and keep on the lookout.

Why do these infectious little creatures travel in gangs?

One theory is that by attacking an organism, they create the weakest link in a chain for others to attack. A feeding frenzy ensues --they are like little piranhas.

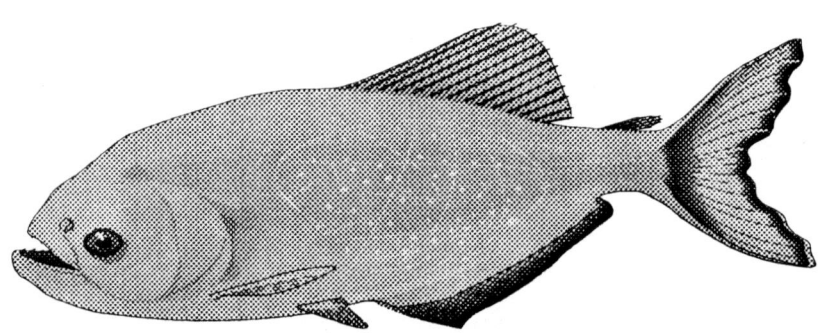

A contrary theory holds that because waste is everywhere and in every system, it should be no big surprise finding the different types of waste together everywhere.

But finally, waste can *cause* and *create* other waste. For example:

- By *overproducing*, all the waste inherent in the system to produce one widget is merely repeated to create more widgets. The same applies to the waste of making *corrections* and the waste of *processing* something for the customer that is not wanted or needed. Unnecessary steps create even more waste.

- By employing *conveyance* waste, we create the need for extra *inventory* to fill our pipeline.

- By waiting, we are often encouraged to just do something. (We don't want to look lazy). So, we *overproduce*? Consume too much *inventory*? *Process* something unnecessary for the customer?

- By using too much *inventory*, we create the extra wastes of *conveyance* and *motion* to handle the excess.

- By exposing ourselves to waste, frustration is created--and the likelihood that we will make mistakes leading to the waste of *correction.*

Waste begets waste.

Detecting and eliminating it will make your environment less friendly to this hostile infection.

Get it before it gets you.

Deductions

The word *deduction* is a double-edged sword. Deductions on your income tax: good. Deductions from your paycheck: bad.

There is, however, another type of deduction, and it refers to the type of logic in which one progresses from a general principle to the specific example.

Lean production is based on deductive logic. This may sound scary, but it's a pretty simple concept.

First we must learn the general principles (the seven types of waste); then we can play Sherlock Holmes and find examples and try to effectively eliminate them.

When these general principles take hold, they will become second nature to us. We can then continuously scan our environment for matches with these general concepts, becoming perceptually more vigilant with practice.

If we do not know what waste is in the first place, we will never be able to detect it.

We will never be able to do more than copy things others have done.

We will be scarcely more knowledgeable than the parrot, who copies without understanding implications.

It seems so logical to travel down this lean production road beginning with the concept of waste. Why then do so many fail to take this route? There are two primary reasons.

First, lean production has many fascinating components each of which can readily draw our attention. Like walking down a circus midway, there are so many interesting things to see that make our minds wander. Attractions become distractions. It's easy to get lost.

All these lean production subsystems, processes, and methodologies, however, exist for one specific purpose: to eliminate waste. Waste is the unifying entity of lean production.

> **Waste** is the common thread that **binds the whole system together.**

Secondly, we are in general an impatient lot who seek action.

Consider that group of teenagers who get bored learning road safety rules in drivers' training.

"Just put me behind the wheel" is their cry.

Perhaps you've run into them on your way home from work. Or worse yet, maybe they've run into you!

If this kind of impatient logic does not get us immediately killed, it ultimately will catch up with us.

So, beginning your implementation of lean production with the study of waste may not be the sexiest, most action-packed approach, but it is the rational, logical thing to do.

Pull in the reins and first learn, then teach, the types of waste. In this system, it is the wisest investment possible.

The rate of return can be phenomenal.

Addressing Waste

The daily periodicals chronicle business's assault on waste. Whether they be "lean production" practitioners or not, they have an intuitive sense of waste's evil effects.

Here are some of the battles that are being fought to eliminate:

THE WASTE OF PROCESSING

❏ The Walt Disney Corporation now processes and pays dividends only once a year in a single check. In many cases, where only a few shares were held, the cost of processing the check exceeded the amount of the check.

❏ Instead of sending monthly condo payments to the condo manager, payments are now sent directly to the bank for deposit.

❏ A recent study showed that 42% of corporate computer projects were abandoned before completion. This electronic technological seduction often ends in breaking off the engagement in hopes of achieving a more rational use of electronic gadgetry.

❑ Federal agencies are attempting to enforce "plain language" in written government communications which is clearer and easier to understand. The challenge is that what they are trying to describe is usually neither clear nor easy to understand!

❑ Cracker Barrel, The Old Country Stores restaurant chain found adjacent to our nation's busiest highways, stopped automatically mailing quarterly results to their shareholders. They are now posting them on their web home page instead, while offering the option to the shareholders of submitting a postcard to request a printed copy.

THE WASTE OF WAITING

❑ McDonald's has taken under consideration the use of a single line queue as used at Burger King and Wendy's as opposed to their "free market system" lines where everyone competes to find the fastest one. HMO's are likewise studying the waiting queues as a response to frustrated customer complaints.

❏ Global Research Systems Inc. is marketing a service using satellite technology to let families know when the school bus is approaching. This is especially helpful in areas with sub-zero temperatures.

❏ Gridlock: A recent study by the Surface Transportation Policy Project showed that nationwide drivers stuck in traffic wasted more than six billion gallons of fuel a year. In addition, when wasted time sitting in stalled traffic was factored in at $11.70 per hour, Washington D.C. drivers incurred the highest annual waste at $1,290 per driver. One potential cause (besides lack of planning) was the waste of correction from not fixing the potholes.

THE WASTE OF CONVEYANCE

❏ One copier company advertises that its machines jam less because their paper path is shorter.

THE WASTE OF OVERPRODUCTION

❑ The book publishing industry is reputed to shred half the books it publishes each year. To combat this, Xerox is offering soft-cover books printed and shipped on demand, based on actual customers' orders.

❑ Books which can be downloaded onto a PC or special "electronic books" are now also on the market, eliminating the need for wasted paper, ink, shipping, inventorying, and storing. With the incredible success of Amazon.com, bookstores are rethinking their traditional need for bricks and mortar.

❑ Made-to-order apparel is expanding from men's dress shirts. Now custom fitting jeans and bathing suits as well as custom made suits can be ordered via the Internet.

❑ New coffee stations can brew one cup at a time in 12 seconds, saving the waste of unused stale coffee. The system also offers a wider variety of choices, including decaf, 50% caffeinated, cocoa, and tea. Just-in-time coffee!

THE WASTE OF MOTION

❑   RFID (Radio Frequency Identification) tags, attached to, or implanted under the skin, can be used to track children, pets, or Alzheimer's patients and keep them from going astray. The technology is also being used to monitor children from getting lost in supermarkets.

❑   Mobil's speedpass method of paying for gas at the pump uses RFID technology, thereby saving the customer the waste of motion going inside the station to pay for the gas.

THE WASTE OF INVENTORY

❑   Computer manufacturers such as Compaq are following Dell and Gateway into the world of making computers on demand. Given their products' short life cycle and high cost, computers sitting on a store shelf and becoming obsolete may be a thing of the past.

❏   Despite rumors of us becoming a paperless society, the number of pages consumed in U.S. offices is increasing at a rate of 20% per year. Most of this increase is coming from printers, and not copy machines.

THE WASTE OF CORRECTION

Progress has been made in allowing the customers to inspect their own orders:

❏   Fast food purveyors are using TV screens at their drive-through so customers can see that their order is correct.

❏   UPS uses a tracking system, so customers can inspect the progress of their packages.

❏   Banks allow their customers to inspect on-line and by telephone the transactions they have posted.

Five Most Important Words

In real estate, the three most important words are location, location, location.

In lean production, the five most important words are:

- Why
- Why
- Why
- Why
- Why

These are known as the *Five Whys*, and when asked in succession can often begin leading down the path to the root cause of a problem. Although known as the Five Whys, it may take only two whys or even fifteen whys to get past the symptoms to the solution.

Unfortunately, in many offices, employees are discouraged from using the word.

OFFICE #1:

Don't ask. That is management's response to many inquiries. The statement immediately arouses suspicion. What are they hiding? What's behind this closed system? Just what is it that authority is not sharing and why? A good place to work? Hmmm.

OFFICE #2

Always ask why. Every time you do something, ask *why* you are doing it. And ask *why* you are doing it the *way* you are doing it.

Office #2 opts for an open system. Because logic is at its foundation, it stands for inspection. It is democratic. The best idea wins. *What's* right is more important than *who's* right. The truth comes first. A much better place to work?

Inspection by means of the Five Whys is not to be feared. It is to be welcomed. The results will make life easier, simpler, and less frustrating.

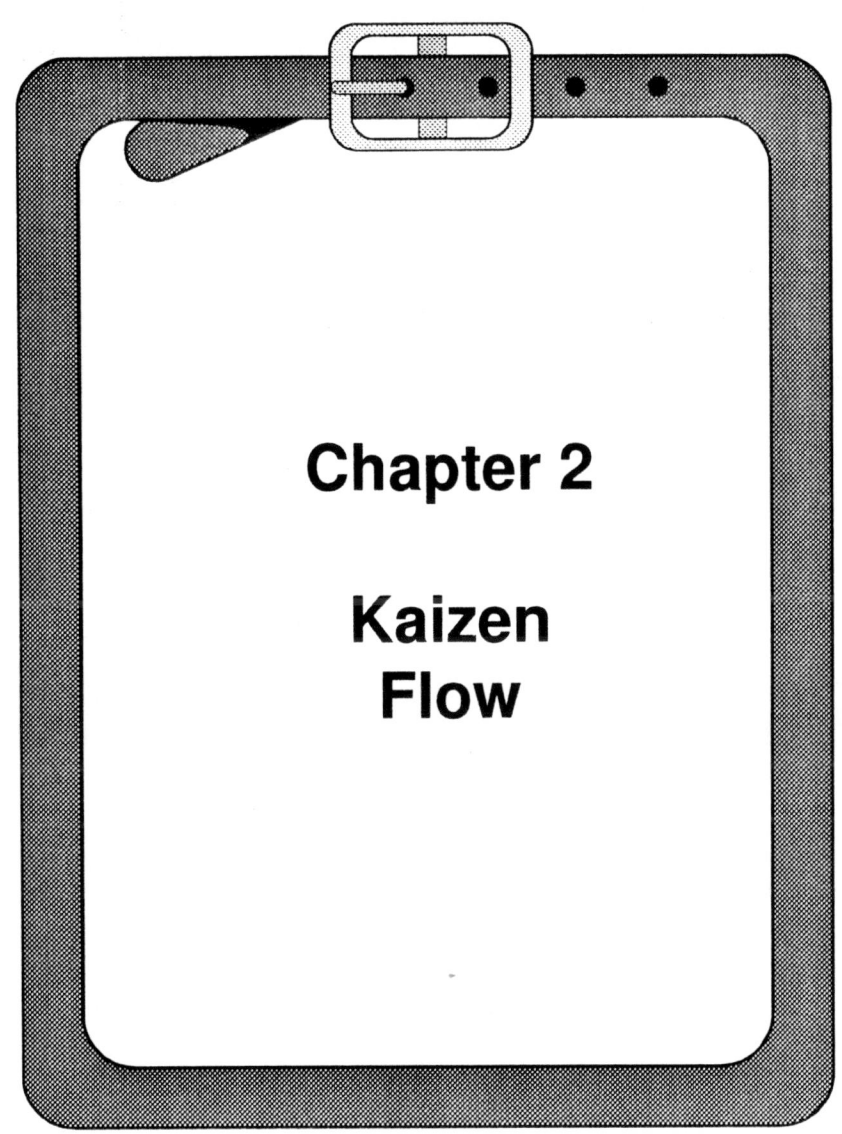

Chapter 2

Kaizen
Flow

The Best Kaizen

When asked the question, "What is the best kaizen?" even many seasoned lean production veterans will answer:

❑ The kaizen that eliminates the most waste.

❑ There is no such thing. Every kaizen is valuable. (This is the democratic approach.)

❑ Small ones are as good as big ones. (Men like this argument.)

❑ The kaizen that provides the most value to the customer.

❑ The one your president likes best. (The politically correct approach.)

The answer to this question, "What is the Best Kaizen?" is

The Next Kaizen!

Why?

Because if there is no next kaizen, continuous improvement dries up. The show's over. Turn out the lights.

Lean production depends on the continuous flow of kaizens, much like a stream of new ideas. When the stream is dammed up, little ingenuity can get through.

It even takes a negative force to stop the flow of kaizens, because they are the product of optimism and hope for a better way to accomplish something.

31

Under the right climate, kaizens multiply like rabbits, and bring more goodies than the Easter Bunny.

In fact, wandering through the office to notice all the newly implemented kaizens is somewhat akin to participating in an Easter egg hunt.

A kaizen is always a *beginning*, not an end. It is the start of a process, and not merely an event.

The next kaizen could be the cure for cancer... or the idea that leads to the idea, that leads to the cure for cancer.

Stifle kaizens at your own risk!

Where Do New Ideas Come From?

Certainly not out of thin air. Not even from the kaizen stork.
Ideas spring from previous ideas. Maybe from just a splinter or
fragment of that idea. Seldom is something created out of nothing.

A recent family reunion inspired the connection between the
family genealogical chart and the evolution of kaizens:

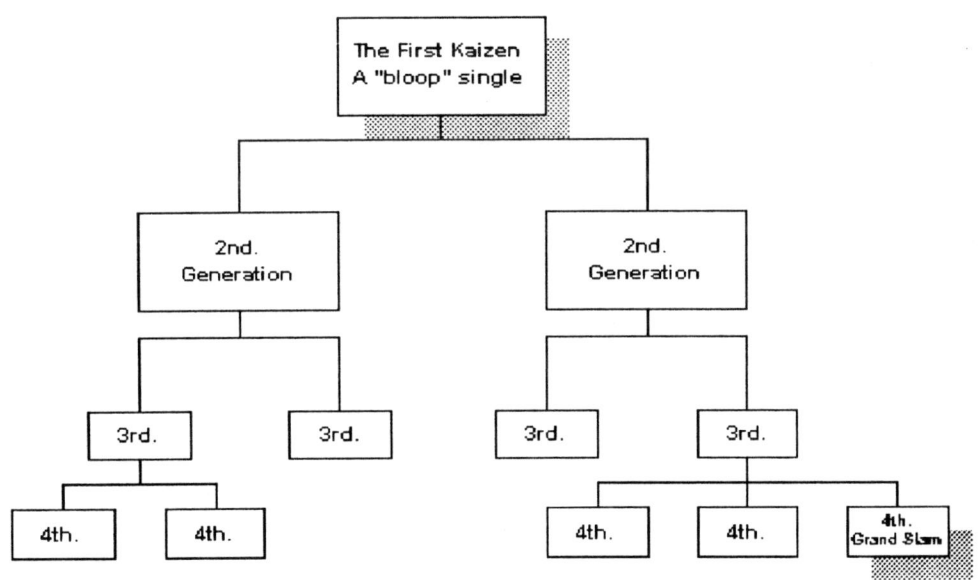

This hypothetical fourth generation "home-run" of an idea was the offspring of a somewhat mediocre idea (bloop single) which was not only allowed, but encouraged to see the light of day.

Yet, how easy it would have been to extinguish that first mediocre kaizen. The excuses--we've heard them before:

- We don't have the time.

- That's small potatoes.

- We're after the big fish.

Between the originating bloop single and the blockbuster home-run idea came many other hits--and some misses. And this story doesn't end with the fourth generation. It will continue to progress in its multiplicative nature ad infinitum--until some force stops the ideas. This idea tree has the capacity to bear much fruit.

As the family tree shows traits passed on from generation to generation, likewise our kaizen genealogy shows that current kaizens carry fragments of ideas from the past. Past remains prologue.

34

Kaizens are by their very nature builders, not destroyers; additive, not subtractive.

Hence, a business culture that encourages and even nurtures new ideas is investing in an intellectual portfolio which can mushroom and grow and create prosperity for many.

In finance, it is known as the power of compound interest. Here, we simply compound ideas and innovation.

"The most powerful principle I ever discovered was compound interest."

Albert Einstein

Oh, Say! Can You See–Kaizens as Visuals

Kaizens serve two purposes.

The first, of course, is to drive continuous improvement; to eliminate waste, thereby driving down costs and allowing your business to remain an on-going entity.

The second purpose is that kaizens serve as seeds for new kaizens. They propagate the species. Success breeds success.

But for these precious
seeds to grow and
bloom, they need light.

Why?

Because a kaizen
that no one sees
will wither and
die on the vine.

Knowing this, the manager must function as a gardener, providing the right climate for the new ideas to develop. One of the gardener-manager's key responsibilities is to create the processes that allow these seedlings to be nourished by the light of day.

One of the easiest ways to accomplish this is to create a bulletin board, exhibiting the latest kaizens.

Can't afford a bulletin board? Create a "virtual" bulletin board as they do at the Technical Liaison Office in Fremont, California, where the Lean Office concept was born. A simple rectangle on the wall created from thin colored tape does the trick. No $150, twenty pound, oak monstrosity needed here, which incidentally has to be bolted to the wall.

To limit the *waste of processing*, limit the kaizen stories to a 3" by 5" card, with the explanation of what was done, which kinds of waste were eliminated, and the identity of the creative artist.

People who come to peruse the board will naturally gravitate to those cards with less print and more pictures, graphs, cartoons–visuals. Words alone tend to intimidate, bore...

Other alternatives to the bulletin board are to:

- Have the employees post the 3" by 5" cards on a wall near their desk. They can be curator of their own kaizen gallery and proudly explain to observers the hows and whys of their ideas. This speaks to the pride of ownership.

- Create a spread sheet showing ideas being implemented by a group or team of employees.

- Use the intra-net to post all the kaizens–arranging them by subject matter or by types of waste eliminated.

- Make new kaizens important features of weekly or monthly staff or department meetings.

Creative, idea nurturing managers will expand greatly on this list.

DON'T COUNT ON IT!

If there is one skill recent college graduates have learned, it is the ability to count.

Bar and line charts abound showing the increasing numbers of kaizens submitted by the willing workers.

What is the purpose of these charts?

- To exhort workers on to even greater numbers? (Or, do they intimidate rather than encourage?)

- To pat ourselves on the back?

- To encourage the executives to continue the kaizen program? This is scary, supposing that top management has only tentatively bought in to the idea in the first place.

The most important thing a visual can give the employee is an idea for his next kaizen. That is a "pull" and not a "push".

Counting kaizens is like counting flowers. Unless you are selling flowers by the piece, it misses the point. One should view and smell flowers.

So before posting that next kaizen bar chart, honestly ask the questions, "Who is the real customer for this information, and why are we sharing it? Will it encourage the flow of kaizens, or hinder it?" Only proceed when you can answer these to your satisfaction.

Getting data is admirable.

But don't count the wrong things.

Stop and smell the flowers.

But resist the urge to count them – as well as the kaizens.

Artificial Respiration

Occasionally, even systems as self-perpetuating as kaizens can slow down and require a boost–akin to putting a little romance back in a marriage.

Short of a pharmaceutical cure, consider the following:

KAIZEN OF THE MONTH

For a given month, recognize all safety or quality suggestions with a cup, hat, t-shirt, or the like. Have one big prize, and draw names from those who submitted suggestions. There might be an increased interest if a trip to the Bahamas is a possible outcome.

WASTE OF THE MONTH

Target one type of waste, e.g., the waste of inventory, and recognize kaizens addressing and eliminating it. A kaizen pin makes a fine memento.

MERIT BADGES

Have a merit badge made for each of your types of waste. Award one to each employee who implements an idea eliminating that kind of waste. Invent your equivalent to a merit badge sash – perhaps a spot on your bulletin board. Make sure they are visible.

Also consider stickers as an alternative. You often see them on the helmets of college football players.

KAIZEN TREASURE HUNT

Hold a contest where participants identify previously implemented kaizens and their suggesters. This brings attention to the changes you've made, and the people behind the good ideas.

What is often needed is
just a shot in the. . .
arm!

As the heart pumps our life's blood through our veins, so must the leadership of an organization be its heart, ensuring the flow of kaizens throughout. Whether this be through creating the culture, serving as a good role model, or by giving occasional booster shots, the resulting new ideas provide the growth and renewal necessary to keep the organism thriving.

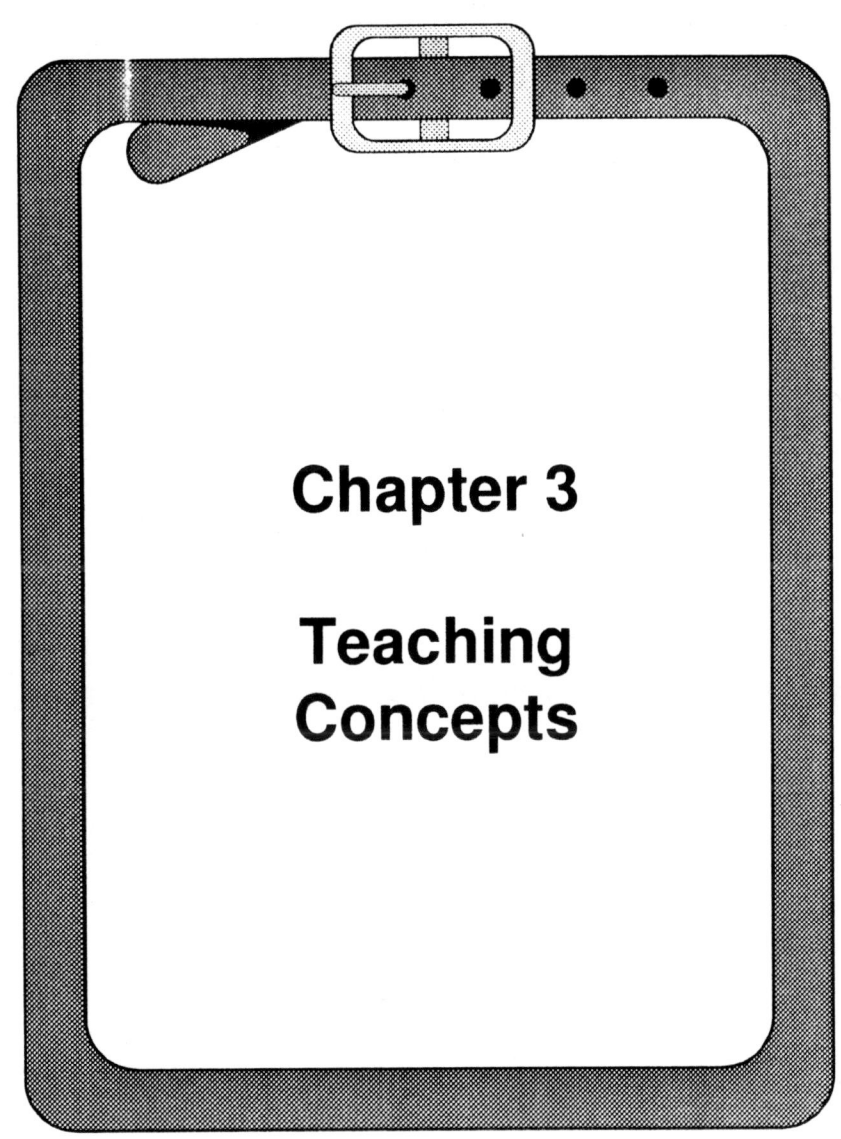

Chapter 3

Teaching
Concepts

The Concept's the thing ...

While chatting with skilled-trades employees engaged in 5S activity, I asked them what they were doing?

Their answer was–"We're doing one of the 5S's; well, it starts with S anyway, that's for sure."

They then tried to remember which "S" it was, sorting, sifting, - but they knew it wasn't sweeping. It was something that began with an "S".

When I further asked them *why* they were doing it, they responded, "Because our supervisor wants us to."

They weren't being flippant - just honest.

Perhaps these obedient employees meant well, but there was little chance of them accomplishing much other than tidying up, especially if their boss wasn't there to directly supervise.

These employees unfortunately were long on specifics and short on concepts. Without a roadmap, they were arguing over whether to turn right or left at a specific corner when they were in the wrong city in the first place!

The **concept** of the procedure (whether it be 5S or something else) is the first and foremost thing a student should be taught: ***Why*** are they doing ***what*** they are doing? Then ***how*** to do it follows next.

Unless this happens, there is little chance they will ever be able to do it on their own–and make some reasonable choices if things don't go according to plan, as usually happens. They are otherwise destined to hit the glass ceiling soon.

This situation was, as usual, a teacher problem and not a student problem. After all, the standard is:

If the student didn't learn, the teacher didn't teach.

So, how should the teachers have approached teaching the 5S? It seems so simple, when we examine the legendary American physicist Richard P. Feynman's teaching philosophy:

"First figure out *why* you want the students to learn the subject and what you want them to know, and the *method* will result more or less by common sense." (The italics are mine.)

Thus, this chapter will be devoted to applying Feynman's simple philosophy of examining why we need to teach which concepts in creating and operating a **Lean Office**.

Grounded with a good understanding of the concepts, the travelers can best navigate through any uncharted territory.

5S Concepts

For an understanding of the simplicity and power of 5S, employees needs to know why it is used. In other words, its *purpose*.

In order to never pass a defect on to the next station in the system, we need to work in an orderly, relatively waste-free environment, that allows us to spot defects easily.

That means our workplace can't be junked up with extra stuff we really don't need. That means we will be able to find things quickly. That means that our work environment will be orderly and clean.

The first three "S's" contain the roadmap of this 5-S concept.

1.   Remove everything unnecessary from your work space.

2.   Arrange what remains.

3.   Clean.

Now, a fair warning: any time a list of three or more things exists, it seemingly attracts an acronym maker. Every organization has one. Unfortunately, the memory device often becomes more important than the concept. Declare this an acronym-free zone.

What is truly important is that the student put the first three S's in his or her **own words**–thereby demonstrating understanding of the concept.

Then they can move on to the details.

The 5S Blessing of the Fleet

Step number one of the 5S is getting rid of clutter in your office or workspace. Everyone you talk to means to do it.

The Southern expression is, "I'm *afixin* to do it". But it seldom gets done. Other, more pressing issues intervene and always out-prioritize it.

During the first step, red tag 5S activity (identifying and labeling the items to go) of my Lean Office Workshop, the reaction usually experienced was:

"I was always going to do this. But I never got around to it. I never had the time."

It is more than the time. When leaders spearhead the red tag activities, it is amazing how much more likely it is that their direct reports join in and discard their clutter.

> When we all red tag together, it is an experience similar to the "Blessing of the Fleet".

It is an activity that is officially sanctioned, and now really O.K. for people to do. How do they know? Because they see their bosses doing it.

In The Lean Office Workshop, participants haul their articles to discard and deposit them in a 5S marshalling pile in the middle of the "U" made by their conference tables.

Workshop participants often look at all the office materials, and immediately react by withdrawing items from the pile that they can use. It reminds one of looting. Then, they pull back, realizing that just because the item may be "free", it might just be relocating junk to their area. On the other hand, it might be getting an item for free that they were just about to requisition. If nothing else, the process gets them to think a little more seriously about how much they really need the item in question.

The word "free" should raise a red flag to all serious 5Sers.

To vegetarians, the dilemma is known as a "free ham".

Remember, you get what you pay for. *Free* may just be another word for, "I'm unloading my waste of inventory on you, sucker".

For those who have seriously and thoroughly decluttered their office or workspace, there is often a great sense of relief that comes from it.

Freedom may ironically be "nothing left to lose".

By blessing the fleet, the action of discarding is sanctioned by the authorizing agent, and the victory goes to the fleet!

Sometimes great journeys can begin with just a little push.

Standardized Work

When a process is done the best, safest, least expensive, fastest, and easiest way, you have achieved a minor miracle.

But even then, to ensure that there is very little variability and that the cake comes out moist, flavorful, beautiful, the same each and every time, is certainly not an easy task.

Standardized work is the tool that makes this possible. It is the road map that leads to the destination.

The key concepts for employees to understand regarding standardized work are:

1)   They must religiously attempt to follow their standardized work.

- It benefits them because it is work done the safest and easiest way.

- It benefits the customer, because it is the best, fastest, and least expensive way.

54

- It adds value for the customer, and thus helps ensure the continuation of the workers' jobs.

2) Standardized work can be changed ...

but not by an individual at his whim. If everyone were allowed to do that, there would be great variability and the quality of the product jeopardized.

Suggestions for change must be reviewed with the supervisor, who can schedule a test or experiment to try out the proposed change, and to see if it is indeed a "better way". If so, the procedure is re-standardized.

There are times and places to express one's individuality. Performing standardized work is not one of these.

Standards – A Moving Target

If everyone achieves a standard, is this good or bad?

Type "B's" argue that in terms of quality, it is indeed good. In fact, nothing beats it.

Type "A's" observe that the only way that it could happen was if the goal were set too low in the first place.

Thus, the question becomes a bit of a Rorschach test, eliciting different answers from different personality types.

"Good" from the nurturing, let's all pull together camp, and "Bad" from the more competitive, we've got to do better side.

As usual, the answer lies with the customer.

Indeed, all processes can and should be continuously improved. But if there is a price involved, the customer needs to be consulted as to whether it is worth it. If the customer does not perceive any improvement, why waste resources on the change? This is the waste of processing.

On the other hand, if a kaizen is inexpensive, yet reduces cost while positively impacting quality, speed, and safety, then implement it immediately. It's a bargain!

Before raising the bar, or improving the standard, we must ask the "why" question ; is it worth it?

One last thought:

If a production standard is 100% achieved, inspect to see if anything was sacrificed to achieve it.

Hopefully, not the truth.

Hopefully, not the quality.

Type "B" concludes: Don't look a gift horse in the mouth.

Type "A" concludes: Beware of geeks bearing gifts.

Leveling

One of lean production's enablers and keys to success is the concept of leveling.

This is the process of flattening the highs and lows of the production schedule. Instead of making ten items on both Monday and Tuesday, twenty each on Wednesday and Thursday, and forty items on Friday, level the process and make twenty each week day.

Otherwise, when there is too much to do, errors are made.

When there is too little to do, mischief appears.

Steady work, with the highs and lows smoothed out is very conducive to high quality, and a less stressed work force.

Those who buy their Christmas or holiday presents all during the year, instead of the night before, know the concept. No dread and panic at the last minute. Fewer mistakes. A sense of calm accomplishment.

Mistakes occur more frequently when an office is over or under scheduled.

How do you go about leveling?

Anticipate and plan. Figure out what in your schedule can be leveled, and what can't.

Then, level what you can.

It's the level headed thing to do.

And, it will level your stress.

Nowhere to Hide

If waste weren't such an effective camouflager, we undoubtedly would have discovered and eradicated much of it long ago. It is a formidable adversary and, as such, should not be underestimated.

This trait leads us to one of lean production's key concepts: transparency–making visible as much as possible.

This includes the good, the bad, and the ugly.

Keep those good things you need to get the job done, your tools, visible. Any time spent looking for them is the waste of waiting.

Your *processes* should also be visible. This allows all employees to inspect and kaizen them. It's very difficult to improve those things you can't see.

As The Godfather once advised, "You should keep your friends close, and your enemies closer." By making your office transparent, you can more easily see all kinds of bad stuff, especially the seven types of waste and defects that may have been produced.

Quickly identifying them can lead to corrective acts which are less intrusive and therefore less expensive to implement.

As far as the ugly, beauty is in the eye of the beholder; and that's no way to think of Mr. Farnsworth, who has been with this firm for over 60 years! Hmm .... we hadn't noticed him much before.

So, how do you create an office where you can find the good, the bad, and the ugly?

You can start by simply looking for incidences of each of the seven types of waste. Play the deduction game.

"Do you have any waste of inventory? Look!"

If you find none, you "Go Fish". Why? Because you know that some waste has to be there. It must be hiding. Look harder and smarter.

Smarter?

Approach this from another angle. If waste is hiding, theorize what it might be hiding behind. What is covering it up?

The general category to consider is anything the opposite of open! Things that can be closed.

What are they?

- Doors
- Desks
- Files
- Computers
- Policy Manuals
- Envelopes

Open these, and you can have a field day identifying and eliminating waste.

It's magic.

Open, says-me!

Let's look at each of these closers (which contains the word losers).

What's to Adore?

What's a Door For?

Doors are two-faced, you say?

Of course!

They have an inside and an outside.

But to find out what they're really up to, we must determine their purpose.

Do they exist for the safety and protection of those who use them, or do they function as nothing more than "walls on hinges"– and primarily aid and abet the forces of that evil, closed storage?

They play "Hide". You therefore, must play "Go Seek".

So while masquerading as mild-mannered, necessary structures, they can often contribute to the cause of waste. They easily hide excess inventory and delay our finding the tools that we need.

Algebraically put:

Door = Kaizen Opportunity

What's a door for?

1)   They keep some things out and some things in.

2)   They keep us from seeing what's on their other side.

Should both reasons apply, one popular kaizen is to put yellow tape on the floor, outlining the door's trajectory. This can alert people so as not to be smacked by a suddenly opening door. Doors to restrooms often are so marked. Swinging doors cause more injuries than might be imagined.

It may be possible for a door to keep people out and at the same time allow the viewing of what's behind it.

It will be difficult for much skullduggery to transpire behind this door.

This bank door shows all!

One bank has solved this problem through the use of an acrylic door, complete with industrial-strength lock. Employees can be easily seen behind the door, thus defeating plans by bank robbers to hide.

When there is no need to impede the motion of people through the opening and no real need to keep people out, the door can simply be discarded or set aside. It has no purpose other than decorative.

Show Me The Way To Go Home

Eliminating doors or making them transparent are two ways to improve them.

A skilled-tradesman at a South Carolina plastics plant came up with an elegantly simple idea for making the door visible in the dark.

Because of the state's harsh weather, his factory often had problems with their electricity going out. To help employees cope with this, he merely painted the jambs of the doors with phosphorescent paint which glowed in the dark.

In the daytime no one would notice or suspect anything out of the ordinary. But at night, or without lights, the doors now serve as navigational aids--beacons in the dark.

This is one place where it is never bad to be caught in a jamb!

Cabinet Doors

On a smaller scale, these doors also keep some things outside and other things inside. If people on the outside can be trusted with what's on the inside, these doors can also go.

More kitchens are moving to open storage. The pantry door has been removed from our kitchen. There's no hiding our food.

See-through kitchen cabinets are becoming more popular, and for ages pots and pans have been hung from the ceiling, out in the open for easy accessibility and use.

The act of making our things visible helps point out that we've got too much in the first place. After all, isn't that part of the reason why we have a tendency to hide it?

Thus, doors are the product of closed storage which is brought about by the waste of too much inventory. Cut down on your inventory, and the necessity or temptation to hide it is eliminated.

If we don't bring stuff through our doors in the first place, the need for doors is diminished. That's Preventative 5S.

This is a system to adore.

Mending Wall

In his poem *Mending Wall*, Robert Frost is reluctant to accept the platitude his neighbor passes down uncritically from his father: "Good fences make good neighbors."

Frost, an early lean thinker, asks "Why?", as there are no cows to contain on either side of the fence by either man.

Frost reasons:

"Before I built a
wall I'd ask to know

What I was walling in
or walling out...

This fence theme followed up an earlier work, *The Tuft of Flowers*, in which a neighbor, arising before dawn, scythes a field, leaving a tuft of flowers, which is much later noticed by a grateful butterfly, as well as by Frost himself, who concludes:

"Men work together..... whether they work together or apart."

There are many varieties of office walls. Full-fledged walls; high cubicle walls; waist-high cubicle walls, as well as intangible walls between departments. Doors, desks, filing cabinets all serve as walls–barricades setting boundaries, confines, limits.

They constitute our bunker--protecting us and our space from others – ironically, those with whom we need to join to accomplish the work at hand.

Instead of mending the wall, we know it needs to be torn down. When The Berlin Wall fell, the world knew it was the right thing to do.

Frost knew there was something that doesn't love a wall.

Yet, resistance to eliminating walls is real. An equilibrium exists between the forces that strain to bring us closer together and those which keep us apart.

The notion that "good fences make good neighbors" persists, and lives uneasily side by side with Frost's realization that we all work together.

So, if wall are bad and flowers are good, then what on earth are wallflowers?

Desks

The first clue that desks mean trouble is that they have doors and drawers: instruments of hidden storage.

The fact that the stuff in them is your stuff makes any 5S argument personal, a direct attack on your values, judgement, and behavior.

The argument that it is *your* desk, and that consequently you should be able to do anything with it (within reason) is a bit specious. It is the company's desk and the company's time you waste looking for the company's inventory stashed therein.

71

So, is there some communal responsibility to keep your desk well organized in the event you are gone and others need to find something quickly?

Or, in a culture that
worships the team,
is your desk that last
vestige and symbol
of individuality?

"It may be a mess, but I know exactly where everything is!"-- that's the common response of the keeper of the messy desk.

Yet empirical data gleaned from casual observation counters this argument. No, these people don't find things quickly, and are often befuddled looking for misplaced items.

As expected, the level of disorganization increases as one travels from the desktop (open storage) to the drawers (closed storage). Even the front of the drawers are more orderly than the back of the drawers, a neverland of items, seldom seen, seldom needed, and seldom used.

But the nagging, recurring fear is that the only action which will make them needed is to dispose of them. Thus they remain huddled, cowering in the darkness of the back of the desk drawer.

Should someone else dispose of these items, it would take the owner months, if ever, to realize they were missing. Yet, such an act would be a violation of our most basic and cherished property rights.

What's the answer?

Some lean offices have gone as far as standardizing desk contents, both on the desk top and in the center desk drawer.

On the desk top, this is accomplished through outlining and labeling the home space for items also used by other office members. Thus when the item is in use, or borrowed, it's absence becomes obvious. Additional, personal items brought in from home are to be kept to a minimum.

Others use a standardized foam insert for the desk's middle drawer. The insert has the outlines of the desk's basic tools carved in it: places for two pens, two pencils, a ruler, pair of scissors, etc. Thus when one needs something from another's desk, he can find, use, and replace it quickly.

Standardizing desk contents clearly affords benefits of reducing waste, but, at the same time, there is a cost to be paid. This cost is in the perceived erosion of the last bastion of office individualism, the sanctity of one's desk.

Most likely you already are wearing standardized clothing, whether or not office members wear official uniforms, they indeed wear unofficial ones.

So, the desk becomes the "hill that we are willing to die on".

Preventative 5S would have us purchase desks with few, if any drawers. (This is the only case when dropping one's drawers would not be considered a violation of sexual harassment laws.)

Eliminating drawers can relocate filing to centralized filing cabinets, which receive greater inspection.

We simply love to collect stuff. It goes back to our hunter-gathering roots. We gather paper and supplies, store them in our desks, then hunt for them. We are **gatherer-hunters**!

Perhaps the best preventative 5S is to eliminate desks entirely.

'Tis best to let employees wrangle with these issues and make decisions that fit the office culture. With the passage of time working in a lean office, employees may feel more comfortable standardizing their desk contents.

To prematurely force them into doing so will likely result in resistance, which can manifest itself in many ways.

It's like squeezing a balloon.

It just bulges out someplace else.

Or worse yet, it may pop.

Squeeze at your own risk!

The "EX-FILES"

Aliens were unquestionably involved in the creation of files and filing. Done to keep earthlings preoccupied "looking up" their stuff, as opposed to looking "up" for other stuff.

Utilizing the wastes of motion, conveyance, and waiting, the aliens figured it would be millennia before they would be discovered.

Filing proved such a huge intergalactic success, incorporating the worst of hidden storage with the anti-5S philosophy of collecting, rather than discarding, that there are plans to use it on other civilizations.

A paranoid fringe group attributes filing as the creation of a secret government agency; but this is highly unlikely, as they have been infected worse than anyone else.

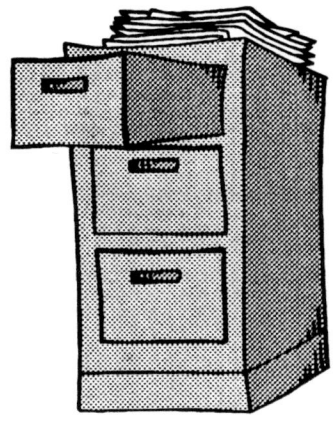

A recent study showed that the average corporate employee is responsible for generating approximately a meter and one-half thick bundle of paper per year, yet during the same time, disposes of only three-fourths a meter.

Regardless of the actual fractions involved, one has to believe we are annually retaining more than we are discarding. The bottom line, however, is that despite our paperless society, paper is indeed expanding, and will eventually crowd us out of house as well as home office.

How do we stop this out-of-control proliferation of paper and filing?

By creating the *Ex-Files!*

SOLUTION #1:

Inspect your files on a regular basis, and discard anything unnecessary: duplicates, outdated materials, things that can be found elsewhere, given the necessity.

Inspecting once a month is good TPM (Total Productive Maintenance). Once a week is better; everyday is best. Level this work by selecting one file to review each and every working day. Go through the file and pull out any unnecessary items. Return these lost puppies to their rightful homes--in many cases, the waste paper basket. Such file reviews will also make you more aware of what you have saved.

Effective 5Ser's begin the first five minutes of each work day doing discarding, organizing, or cleaning. This time could be used to 5S just one file.

Another useful technique which better yet levels your Ex-Filing work is the LIFO system. Anytime you file a piece of paper, remove one or two pages from the files. Removing one page ensures a "no-growth" policy; two or more pages will result in a gradual reduction.

While this may seem painful, filing should be painful. Hiding things is seldom good, especially in a lean production environment. Even squirrels, for the most part, can't find most nuts they've hidden. That's why they bury so many! Maybe that's why we make and file duplicate copies?

Efficiency experts tell us that our paperwork problems are merely a reflection of our inability to make decisions. Most advise that there are only three or four things to do when a new piece of paper comes across our desk:

1) Act upon it.

2) Give it to someone else (tag - you're it).

3) Throw it away immediately.

4) File it.

Category four, filing, is technically done for preservation or future reference.

More than likely, however, filing is actually done because we 1) don't know what action to take; 2) who to give it to; and 3) we are afraid to discard it. Thus instead of intentionally preserving it or keeping it for future reference, filing merely results as a default option - "Not Capable of Making a Decision".

SOLUTION #2:

The *best* solution to destroy the alien life form of bulging, pulsating files is through **Preventative 5S**: Don't file it in the first place.

With each piece of paper about to be filed, give it the FBI Interrogation:

1)   Why am I filing you?

2)   Is there any reason I shouldn't destroy you right now? What's the worst thing that could happen if I do?

Filing is like a rampant disease and spreads waste. The more paper in your files, the more you have to look through to find things- thereby the wastes of motion, conveyance, and waiting. The more you file, the more you hide, and the more you create waste.

Increased files (soft-ware) lead to the purchase of more hardware (the metal files). Then, the cycle spirals out of control and empty file drawers attract new files like moths to a flame. (Whoever left an empty file drawer empty?) File cabinets are enablers for the insidious disease of filaholism. Files are magnets for papers.

The word *file*, is actually derived from the Latin phylum, meaning--"Hide this crap, fast!"

Phile (silent "p") is also defined as a fondness or affinity for something. That's a kind way of saying it's addictive. Yet the evil filing industry has kept that from the public for years, even hooking small children on color-coding, once they learn their colors.

Only through the 5S can one achieve redemption and "Ex-Filer" status.

FOR HELP:

Twelve step groups can be found in most phone directories. Two step groups can be found in most country and western bars.

But the group you want are those focused 5S-ers who both practice preventative 5-S and resist the urge to retain and file in the first place, and vigilantly seek outdated files to discard.

The lesson: get files before they get you.

This has been a public service announcement.

The truth was in here.

The Telephone

The phone is a tool with the ability to help us like no other. In times of danger, dialing "911" can make the difference between life and death.

When we call others, it can save on the wastes of motion, conveyance, and waiting.

When others call us, it is quite a different thing.

ON-LINE: When we answer others' calls, we can either offer immediate service to a customer, or allow others to impose their priorities on our schedule. Answering the phone can be a two-edged sword. Caller ID provides some technology to help us sort out which calls are vital.

OFF-LINE: With **voice mail**, we can capture all our messages, prioritize them, and respond at our discretion and convenience. The same applies to **e-mail**. The problem lies with the waste of inventory--we can easily get deluged with messages.

For as frustrating as they can be, remember that prior to the phone and telegraph, messages traveled at "the speed of horse"--and with the phone, there's no cleaning up!

Computers

Computers are marvelous, now commonplace, machines which perform three primary functions:

1. They compute data at fantastic speeds.

2. They transmit data at rates approaching the speed of light.

3. They can store giant quantities of data.

From a lean aspect, two out of three aren't bad. The computer's great speed allows us to reduce the wastes of waiting and conveyance.

But, the hidden storage of data is not something to be welcomed. Even with the cost of electronic storage coming down significantly, it is still an unwise habit to develop.

Because the data is hidden, it remains difficult to access by anyone other than the computer operator to whom the data belongs.

As with paper files, TPM and preventative maintenance must be performed on the computer files.

The same tips given to keep paper files in check apply to e-files:

●   5S must become a regularly practiced activity.

●   Preventative 5S remains the best cure.

Just because we have the capacity to store data doesn't mean that we should. Because real estate was cheap, we built huge factories. Because gas was cheap, we built huge cars.

Computer magazines regularly list suggestions on how to clean off your hard drives to free up more space:

Some current examples are:

- Uninstall extra fonts you don't use.

- Uninstall Window applications you will never use.

- Uninstall any other applications you never use.

On a regular basis:

- Delete old e-mail, both sent and received.

- Delete your Internet cache file.

- Select and delete files with the endings: .bak, .old, .log, .tmp, .ckk

- Eliminate one letter file each time you write a letter.

As computer technology rapidly changes, so will these suggestions.

Frequently peruse computer magazines for helpful tips.

Policy Manuals

Policy manuals are the Rodney Dangerfields of business. They just don't get any respect.

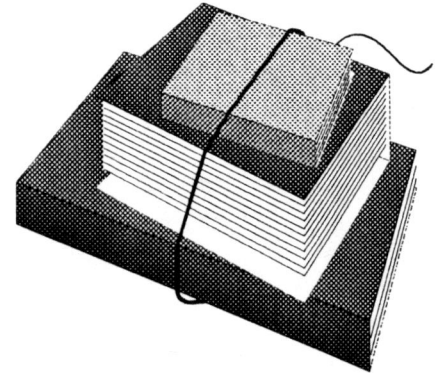

Their intent is good--to standardize procedures, thus ensuring quality in carrying them out.

With each successive reorganization comes an assault on the old organization's policies and procedures. This, in itself, is probably not a bad thing to do. The procedures should see the light of day more often.

The best way to rate the policy manual's effectiveness as a tool is to give it "the 3 E test". Is it:

1)   Easy to see?

2)   Easy to use?

3)   Easy to return?

1)   Most policy manual material is stashed away in three ring binders, making it difficult to see.

2)   Its content is of such prodigious thickness that it becomes intimidating to use, no matter how well it is indexed.

3)   Its ease of return is probably its best asset. After lugging it to your desk, you can't wait to return it as soon as possible.

Two changes would make policy manuals incredibly more effective:

●   Condense them to one page in length on standardized work forms.

●   Post them near their point of use.

Then as tools they will become much more useful, used, and able to be scrutinized for kaizening.

Then they will get more respect.

And the Envelope, please.....

Envelopes and the mailing process in general offer great opportunity for kaizen.

That's because envelopes not only conveniently store things for delivery, but they also conceal their contents.

Companies deal with this challenge by:

● Asking the customer to review a check list printed on the back of their billing envelope to ensure the correct items are returned:

1. The check is enclosed, signed, and has the account number on it.

2. The return address is showing through the cellophane window in the envelope.

3. The required portion of the bill is enclosed.

- Ameritech further warns us, through the use of the international icon (a red circle with a slash through it) not to use staples or paperclips.

While these help assure the fastest processing of the materials when they arrive, there is a better way, which is to avoid the use of the envelope all together, and participate in the electronic bill paying system.

- Almost a decade ago, my assistant was surprised to find that using a windowed envelope was actually cheaper than taking the time to retype the addressee's name and address on a plain white envelope. As we responded to hundreds of resumes a year, this saved much time and energy, by eliminating the retyping of the name and address.

Today many companies respond to inquiries through the use of e-mail. Some, unfortunately, use e-mail to inform interviewees of the outcome of their interview. Very poor manners.

Before focusing on the envelope for kaizen, however, the communication process itself should be examined. First and foremost:

- Is there really a need for this communication? If not, discontinue it and see what happens.

- Is there another, better way to communicate the message that is faster, less expensive, and time consuming? Perhaps merely updating your web-site can accomplish this.

Because of their tendency to hide things, opaque envelopes should be one of the first casualties of the transparent office.

Practicing 5S, standardized work, and breaking down the walls that hide the waste in your office will not only increase the wellness of your processes and procedures, but also the attitude, morale, and enthusiasm of your employees.

That aspect of lean production seldom gets the attention it deserves.

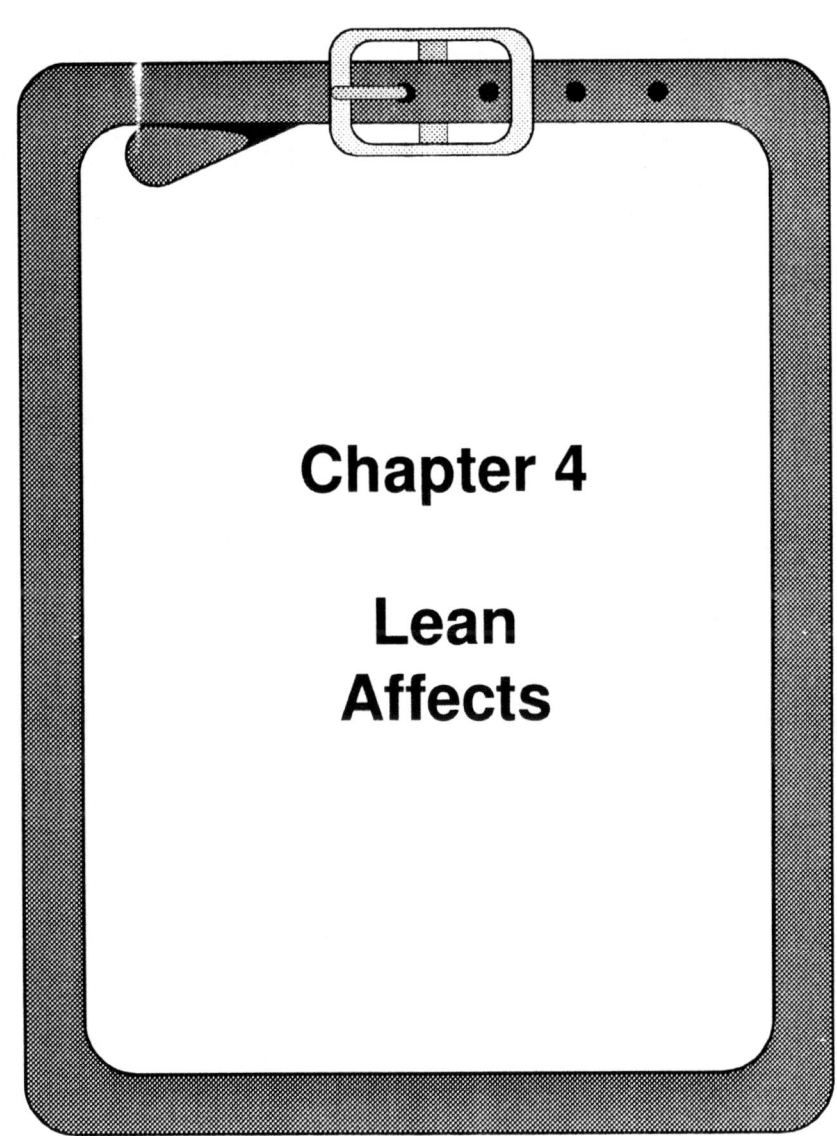

Chapter 4

**Lean
Affects**

Effects and Affects

The *effects* of business decisions are the sought-after results we hope to attain through the choices we make. They are typically measurable goals: increase sales by 20%, up net income by 7%.

The *affects*, or emotional impacts of the same decisions, however, are seldom given more than passing consideration or lip service. They are not as easily measured, and hence often considered less credible.

Lean production employed in the office or in the manufacturing environment, or both, most likely will make a sizable positive impact on employee morale. Those who have experienced the change never want to return to the old way of doing things.

A culture where employees are positive and continuously seek ways to make things better is an incredible bonus just for implementing a new way of making things.

This chapter contains vignettes about lean production's impact on people, and how it makes them *be* and *feel* a vital part of the change.

It is foolish to dismiss such substantive qualitative changes because of quantitative difficulties in counting or measuring them. With ingenuity, they can be measured. But at some level, one should ask why? What are the opportunity costs spent in doing so?

Exploring lean's affective side leads us to:

- The virtues of participation.

- Improving processes to improve results.

- Humor in the workplace.

- Human Resource's contribution.

- Fulfilling needs--Maslow's Hierarchy.

- Recognition and reward for reinforcement.

- Support for the operator.

The Joy of Participation

At a report-out session of a large automotive supplier, administrative employees from all levels of the company took turns addressing the assembled group, updating them on the kaizens they had either implemented or were in the process of implementing.

There was great excitement throughout the room about the new ideas. Even formerly skeptical or cynical employees had caught the fever and were sharing their clever contributions on how to eliminate waste. Those who would have previously been considered cynical had been transformed into leaders. Negatives to positives.

The President of the company now loved to conduct tours of his headquarters, encouraging his employees to explain their contributions to the cause.

Employee affect had changed. The atmosphere was now more positive. Happier. Friendlier. Funnier.

How does one put a value on this? What's it truly worth?

When Did Low Morale Become Fashionable?

Since re-engineering and downsizing frenzies gripped industry in the 1980's, employees' feelings have become disregarded, if not completely ignored. They have become the absolute bottom of the food chain.

Yet, when bully CEO's get sent packing, workers at all levels across the country react with glee. The wicked witch is dead!

How could business have gotten so cruel and greedy that a nickname like "Chainsaw Al" could be considered a moniker of strength--or a sign of the toughness needed to make the hard decisions. What were we thinking?

Companies which use lean production techniques in their offices or their manufacturing concerns are companies that have made the decision to concentrate on improving their processes as a way to get better results. For the emotional health of employees as well as stockholders, this is a good thing.

Process vs. Results

We've been led to believe that there are two ways to get things done in business.

You can be process-oriented, focusing on the process and letting the results take care of themselves.

Or, you can go straight to the results, and invest your energy strictly on the bottom line, demanding more, better, faster!

Such arguments miss the point. This is not vanilla vs. chocolate. There is a rainbow of flavors and combinations, not to mention swirled chocolate and vanilla.

As important as improving processes is to lean production, to be forced into a corner arguing that results aren't important is not where one wants to be. It is not wise strategy. Suicidal, really.

Without results, Darwinian forces will soon have your company sinking in a tar pit.

Results are those flashing lights on the scoreboard indicating how competitive you are. They are not only a report card, but feedback reflecting on your processes.

By focusing on processes as a way to improve the results, lean production accomplishes this with less screaming, blaming, rework, delay, and waste and more camaraderie, teamwork, problem solving, and focus.

When you have poor processes, working harder will seldom lead to the desired results.

Buying ten lottery tickets instead of one does increase your odds, but only infinitesimally, and at *ten times the cost*, which is immediate. That cash could go somewhere else more fruitful.

"Results-only" managers can threaten all they want, but running faster down the wrong path won't get you to your destination more quickly. Ironically, it can take you farther away.

There is truth in the old saw:

If you keep doing what you've always done, you'll keep getting what you always got.

Managers who have seen the lean production system work have faith that over time great processes will produce great results.

This may say more about empirical data predicting expected outcomes rather than about faith. Then again....

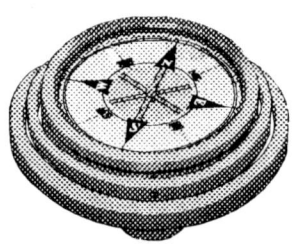

Humor in the Workplace...
Or - Excuse Me – I Forgot to Laugh

In the first five minutes of the typical **Star Trek** episode, we are introduced to brand new, squeaky-clean, crew members with the talent and idealism to take the Starship Fleet successfully into the next millennium.

Don't be fooled. They are the *expendables*--mere alien-chow for some grotesque extra-terrestrial who, shortly after consuming them, is found only to have needed some simple kindness, understanding, and alternative source of protein.

Today, many corporate as well as public sector employees feel like expendables. With downsizing, rightsizing, reengineering, and resultant outplacement, it is no wonder that stress is up, laughs down.

Workplace humor now tends toward cynicism.

Knock-knock.

Who's there?

You aren't!

Expendable, indeed!

So, how does the marketplace react to our angst?

A "workplace-humor" industry has sprouted in the form of books, web-sites, and stand-up comedian/consultants. Generally speaking, they do provide a few immediate laughs. And more humor inherently seems better than less humor. When management brings these people in to entertain the weary troops at the corporate banquet, laughter soon fades to feelings of having been manipulated.

We are better served by asking the question "Why are people successfully selling the concept of more humor in the workplace?"

By continually asking the why questions, we can approach the problem's root cause--which points to increasing stress levels, brought on by:

- Spending too many hours away from the family.

- Performing two jobs previously handled by three employees.

- Dealing with a supervisor who doesn't listen.

- Being manipulated by *team-speak.*

- Being appraised by a boss who not only doesn't know what you do, but who hates to do appraisals in the first place.

- Being underpaid.

Humor allows us to cope and temporarily relieve these negative stresses, but it does nothing to get to the root cause of the problem.

Humor is now often used at work just as singing was used in the cotton fields.

So, is Workplace Humor an oxymoron?

Or is your supervisor just a plain old moron?

(Now that's cheap humor used to reduce stress!)

But look what happens when:

- Supervisors are there for the support and not just the control of their employees.

- Employees are not only listened to, but their ideas are expected everyday to continuously improve the work processes.

- There is adequate training.

- There is realistic hope for advancement.

- There is trust and respect.

- There is adequate pay.

Humor in this environment is going to be different than humor in the typical workplace.

It is the difference between humor as *joy* and humor as **stress-relief**.

Honest laughter. In the workplace. What a concept.

Did I ever tell you the one about how many supervisors it takes to screw in a light bulb?

Memo to the Human Resource Department: Lend Me Your Tired, Poor, Huddled Masses...

Fifteen years working in a human resources department for a giant manufacturer, the last two of which were spent observing the HR function of a Toyota-run facility, led me to the following conclusions about the impact of lean production on the human resources activity:

In the old mass production environment, the HR department spent much time and energy patching up employees to send them back into battle.

Whether attending to their physical needs in the medical, benefits, or safety departments, or to their psychological needs through counseling or discipline, or even by devising reward, recognition, or appraisal programs, one always had the sense that we operated as a corporate MASH unit attending to the wounded.

Critics often accused our HR activity as being "keepers of the bureaucracy".

Prior to my assignment at NUMMI, I was assigned the managerial duties for the company's suggestion program, an opportunity to implement continuous improvement.

Many employees had complained that the rejection letters they received were not convincing, and lacked adequate explanations as to why their suggestions were rejected. Thus, I decided to focus on improving suggestion investigation.

So, I first retrained suggestion investigators. I then walked the extra mile by getting up at 4 a.m. to spend the time to craft humane rejection letters from the now better-documented reports of the suggestion investigators.

At the time, this was regarded as a big improvement in the suggestion program. HR was taking one more step to meet the needs of its workers.

Looking back, the effort was less successful than trying to teach a pig to sing.

The suggestion investigators resented the extra work spent to better document the suggestions from people in other departments who didn't have a clue in the first place of the processes involved.

The suggesters, who were receiving rejections at the rate of 95%, didn't really want better explanations for their rejections. They just didn't want to be rejected so often!

The employees participated in a system where they were not allowed to submit suggestions relating to their own job. Suggestion awards were very large, contributing to the prevailing opinion that it was their responsibility to make improvements in their **own** processes. To win an award, they had to make suggestions in another person's area. Needless to say, they were often considered interlopers. And even if they had a good idea, it wasn't invented *here*. Perhaps a 5% acceptance rate wasn't bad, given the circumstances.

'Tis so clear, looking back. It was the system that was wrong. Working harder within the system would only provide marginal results.

On the other hand, in the lean production environment I observed at NUMMI, the HR function existed to support the lean production system.

Their suggestion activity, one of the best in the country, promoted participation and communication through rewarding employees for smaller suggestions relating to their own jobs or to processes of which they were knowledgeable. The rewards were usually nominal, usually in the range of $9 - $30.

Their acceptance rate matched my experienced rejection rate! In addition, my program had a minimum suggestion reward of $50. The majority of their successful suggestions were not eligible for our plan.

In our suggestion activity, which occasionally gave out rewards in the thousands of dollars, employees complained it still wasn't enough. Other employees complained that a winning idea was theirs, and not the opportunist's who beat them to filling out the suggestion form. The more money involved, the bigger the arguments. Never had so much money been paid to tick-off so many employees!

The two different suggestion systems reflect a difference in philosophy and purpose.

In the one, the human resources function administered the Band-Aids and sent the soldiers back to war.

In the other, the HR function armed their employees to fight not against their own system, but within it to improve it and produce the best products they could.

WORKING HARDER – LIKING IT MORE

Production line employees at NUMMI who had worked under both types of systems in the same plant, chose lean production by an overwhelming majority, even though they admitted to working much more consistently, if not harder, under lean production. Favoring a system where they *physically* worked harder said a lot about its perceived *psychological* benefits.

To understand these, we turn to motivational theory.

Since the 1940's, many motivational theories have come and gone, but one has had a lasting impact due to its simplicity and believability: Abraham Maslow's *Hierarchy of Needs*.

The Pyramid

Abraham Maslow posited that man by nature is a needy animal. His behavior reveals that he fulfills these needs according to their level of importance and urgency to him. Generally speaking, if man is famished, he will seek food before questing for higher order needs such as love and self-esteem.

Maslow defined his hierarchy as five levels of needs. They are commonly represented as rising from the base of a pyramid.

At the base are the **physiological** needs. Man will attempt to meet these needs to fulfill his need for food, water, sleep, oxygen, sex, etc. They are critical to his self-preservation.

Secondly, moving up the pyramid, is his need for **safety**. This transcends not only staying alive, but obtaining a feeling of security, orderliness, and a sense of the predictability of his environment.

The third need is for **love**. That can also be defined as his needs for affiliation.

Fourth, is **esteem**. Self-respect, achievement, and recognition all make their entrance here.

At the top of the pyramid is **self-actualization**. This is often characterized as what motivates artists, musicians and writers to create. These are people who come close to reaching their full potential.

So, how do the affects of lean production fit with the five levels of Maslow's Hierarchy?

PHYSIOLOGICAL NEEDS

One could argue that by using lean production, a business is more likely to remain viable, and thereby better able to continue to provide the employees' wages which can be used to procure the basics of food and shelter. That's a stretch, as both systems meet man's basic physiological needs.

SAFETY NEEDS

Maslow defined safety not in the OHSA sense of the term, but as a peaceful environment, characterized by the safety of a mother's arms; no extremes; no wild animals to gobble you up; no quarreling; no divorce; a sense of protection or insurance.

Here is where lean production excels, providing a secure psychological safety-net by creating a predictable, organized, orderly environment.

- 5S provides the order and the workplace organization, lack of clutter and cleanliness.

- Standardized work provides the structure to reduce the variability of the processes.

- Waste Elimination provides a system to continually remove the unnecessary and always frustrating components of waste.

- Kaizens provide the opportunity for continuous improvement and hope.

- Visual Management provides the means to eliminate the confusion and frustration inherent in poor communication.

Lean production provides the tools to ensure a predictable outcome. Few surprises. Any disruptions are but problems to be calmly solved.

LOVE NEEDS

Love is defined in this instance as affection or a sense of belongingness.

By eliminating waste through reducing the chance for errors, and by providing the tools to deal with them when they do occur, much frustration and anger are driven from the people operating within the system. But absence of anger does not equal love.

By placing employees in small teams, where each person's performance is vital for the team's success, the environment is created for individuals to see and value each other's skills and contributions. Respect and good-manners fit naturally in this environment.

The system is designed to provide the team culture, the tools, and methods to succeed, and the consequential operative effect (and affect) is one of predictability and hope.

ESTEEM NEEDS

When the organization provides the needed support, employees can act like and be treated like adults, with confidence and self-respect.

Praise is empty unless it is perceived as deserved for a specific, appropriate, action.

The core philosophy recognizes people as organisms that inherently make mistakes. Rather than expend energy on blaming and chastising, the energy is spent instead on creating an environment that precludes mistakes. Error-proofing, visual management, standardized work, the 5S all help keep the individual freer from mistakes. And when a mistake does occur, the system provides the ability to detect it quickly, and stop the process (jidoka) in order to fix it quickly and surely.

When behavior meets standards, self-esteem is not far behind.

SELF-ACTUALIZATION NEEDS

The apex of Maslow's pyramid is held by self-actualization, a sense of approaching the nearly infinite potential man can achieve. Often considered obtainable by obsessed artists who travel to the beat of a different drummer, self-actualization sounds somewhat far-fetched to be applied to manufacturing or to the office.

Yet there is a transcendent skill in doing any job both large and small to the very best of one's abilities. The door remains open.

Comparing the *affects* of lean production to those of mass production is difficult, because the emotional culture in mass production can vary so much.

By employing the characteristic sub-systems of waste elimination, kaizen, 5S, and standardized work, lean production tends to lessen the variability of affect from one location to another. Good affect comes with the "package".

By re-examining lean production in light of Maslow's Hierarchy, it's easily seen that a great part of lean's *effectiveness* comes from its *affectiveness.*

It goes a long way toward meeting the safety, love, and self-esteem needs of employees, which are often over-looked or merely disregarded by other systems or methods.

It not only works right.

It "feels" right.

Reinforcement

What? Back-ups coming to help me? You've got to be kidding.

No, reinforcement is just a B. F. Skinner concept of explaining why people and other animals behave the way they do. Skinner concluded that if we reward behavior immediately after it occurs, presto, the frequency of that behavior increases. So simple. So powerful.

Conversely, when behavior is not rewarded, it tends to disappear, or extinguish.

So, reinforcement is like the gas pedal on a car. It makes things go.

But not always in the direction we intend.

Where we end up depends not only on how hard we hit the accelerator, but also on how well we steer the car.

Corporate recognition programs, whether intended to be or not, are reinforcement programs.

They are the kinder, gentler form of control favored over the more familiar confrontation or coercion. The carrot over the stick.

BE CAREFUL WHAT YOU REWARD; YOU'LL GET MORE OF IT!

My initial contribution to an executive board session was questioning a motion to recognize, as an example of fine teamsmanship, the efforts of an Australian employee who worked through a weekend to solve a plant problem, thereby foregoing a vacation his family had planned and counted on for months.

I noted that while this was indeed, exceptional, it was certainly not an example of fine teamwork.

An excellent team would have used standardized work to cross-train its other members, who would have stepped in to solve the problem together, and let their teammate and his family take their well-deserved holiday.

There was dead silence. The president, who was clearly annoyed, suggested we move on with the agenda.

I had completely missed the point. Giving up one's vacation was precisely the behavior revered by the company's top executives. Sacrifice. Laying down of one's body for the success of the company.

The fact that they had labeled it "teamsmanship" was irrelevant and immaterial.

They indeed knew the power of recognition and reinforcement. Labeling sacrifice "team work" was a fine bit of verbal manipulation, akin to something out of Orwell's _Animal Farm_.

WHY IS RECOGNITION FEARED?

Human resource literature extols the virtue of increasing the use of recognition, suggesting that recognition shouldn't be limited to just the top five per-cent of employees. Everyone can benefit by it. We all know we could!

But, apparently, hitting the accelerator and steering at the same time are much more difficult than one would suspect.

The problem is that when you reward one thing, you elect by default not to reward another. What happens to the behavior of those not rewarded? Are they selfless in their joy for their fellow employees' recognition, or are they silently jealous and embittered by the unfairness of it all?

Dangerous stuff, this being nice and recognizing people. As the road to hell is often paved by good intentions, there is more than meets the eye in why recognition isn't used as much as predicted.

Effective recognition needs to be sincere, fair, consistent, timely, frequent, flexible, appropriate, specific, and done privately or publicly as the situation requires.

And, whenever recognition is part of a contrived program, by nature it becomes less sincere.

So, to begin, it is vital to choose carefully those things you wish to reinforce. Reinforcing too many things will cause confusion.

In a lean production environment, recognition is afforded to two prime values: submitting and implementing new ideas, or kaizens, and having exemplary attendance. Both positively impact quality and cost.

But before racing to implement a recognition system, it is important to carefully consider what specific kinds of behavior are desirable, wanted, and therefore to be reinforced.

For example, would you rather see 100 kaizens from one team member than ten each from each of the eight team members? If the total numbers are the important factor, then the century kaizen person should be "suggestor of the year".

If, on the other hand, you want to use the program to get everyone involved, rewards should reinforce the highest percentage of participation, thereby encouraging everyone to join in the continuous improvement fun.

This fits with the concept that the best kaizen is the next kaizen. Two of the key goals of the Toyota suggestion program are to increase communication and teamsmanship. This is accomplished by encouraging *everyone* to get involved.

If the suggestion program's emphasis were put on the size of the suggestion's savings and the size of the reward assigned, the system would create fewer, but more handsomely rewarded employees and far more cynical and jealous ones.

Ironically, spending more money may bring on bigger problems. Good intentions and reinforcement systems begin walking down the same path together, but often get separated in transit.

TIMING IS EVERYTHING

If exemplary attendance is something to be rewarded and reinforced, then yearly perfect attendance awards should be reconsidered. Why? Because an employee who misses just one day in the year is out of the running. Most people get sick one time a year and should not bring their infectious diseases to work, endangering the health of others.

Even in baseball, it's not one strike and you're out!

Thus, why not give smaller recognitions, pins, luncheons, free food, to employees who had perfect attendance for the last quarter?

If attendance rewards are truly reinforcing, which will lead to the more sought after behavior? Once a year recognitions, or quarterly recognition?

Actually, the argument needn't be an either/or option, as you can give an extra award to anyone with four consecutive quarterly rewards, instead of going by calendar year. It's a small price to pay for such a huge benefit.

When I was at NUMMI, the UAW president proudly displayed his seven years of perfect attendance pins on his cap.

Both union and management knew the value of the employees and the importance of their being at work every day possible.

Wreck-Cognition

In a parallel universe there exist bosses who not only eschew the use of recognition, but instead use its evil twin, ***wreck-cognition***.

It has a sinister, effective ability to humiliate and discourage employees, and is characterized by:

- Failing to recognize exemplary accomplishments over and above the call of duty.

- Failing to recognize steadiness and consistency most often taken for granted when doing a tedious job.

- Singling out an individual for recognition when a group or team really deserved the credit.

- Making recognition public and consequently embarrassing the recipient.

- Making recognition private when it should have gone public.

- Giving recognition inappropriate for the job done.

- Damning with faint praise.

Take a moment and reflect on those repressed memories of when you were the victim of ***wreck-cognition***. It's happened to all of us.

Learn from these examples. You can do better.

Especially in a lean environment, encouragement is vital to keeping the kaizens flowing from ***all*** members of your organization.

Every garden needs a climate conducive to growth. Do your part to keep the sun shining.

Phony Sincerity

Recognition often fails because it simply lacks the human element.

Recognition rests, above all, in the *eye of the beholder*. So, if one does not know the recipient, chances for poor results increase. The recipient has to cherish the acknowledgement or gift for it to be effective. As people don't all value the same things, this is not a time to guess.

Secondly, recognition needs to come from the heart.

It needs to be sincere.

A professor of abnormal psychology once told our class the way to create a psychotic was through the use of double-bind messages.

CHAPTER 4
The Joy of Participation

The cold mother calls her child to her, asking for a hug, then stiffens and gives the child the iciest kiss imaginable, at the same time asking "What's the matter, don't you love your mother?" Joan Crawford could have played that role superbly.

Only real human beings can give recognition effectively. Icy mothers needn't even try.

There's just no faking it!

Just-in-Time Recognition

The definition of lean production: delivering the right thing, in the right amount, at the right time, at the right place ironically also applies to the concept of recognition.

Wreck-cognition occurs :

- when we say the wrong thing; or even when we say the right thing, but say too much or too little.

- when we say it at the wrong time or the wrong place.

- when we are insincere.

- when we try to be too cute.

Recognition, like lean production, needs to be just-in-time.

Support For the Operator

In the typical business organization, supply and demand dictate that the most valuable people are near or at the top of the organization chart pyramid. They are highly skilled, hard to replace, and paid well relative to the organization's other members.

In a lean production environment, it is virtually the same, except that the organization chart is turned upside down, and the wide end of the pyramid is at the top.

Such an organization exists to support its operators, or the people who manufacture its product, be they on the shop floor or behind a computer screen.

The reason: this is where the most value is added to the product. What matters is no longer the manager's ***span of control***, but the manager's ***span of support***.

Let's face it. The customer doesn't give a rip if you just got promoted to Assistant Cost Accounting Manager. The customer doesn't even care who your department heads, vice-presidents, or even presidents are.

All they care about is the person or persons putting your product together. They hope they are well and doing a fine job. They hope they are well selected, well trained, and well supported to consistently perform their tasks.

How well these people perform their tasks reflects on the whole organization.

But when the person "on-the-line" is regarded as just a small cog in the machinery--just a grunt, chances are the customer will be thought of in the same class.

White-collar perks are often the first casualties when implementing lean production. This should only be a problem with unenlightened managers, who will begin to stick out like sore thumbs.

No longer is there a need for fancy offices. In fact, open offices provide the greatest transparency, allowing all facets of your processes to be seen.

There is no need for executive dining rooms, as they prohibit the operators at the top of the pyramid from giving informal feedback to those who support them in their quest to provide the best for the customers.

Fancy clothes and ties are no longer needed to distinguish the supervisors from the supervised. Team golf shirts and jeans or Dockers make great corporate uniforms. Clothing is non-value added, and shouldn't even merit discussion during the day. There are much more important things to talk about. Public schools have begun to learn this lesson from their private school competition.

What results is a truly more democratic environment, to which most will respond favorably.

There will be some white-collar employees who are very threatened by the removal of these perks. They need some time to adjust and join the team.

But if they can't adjust over time, they will be happier elsewhere. In this case, it's best for them to part company.

A ship can only drag
an anchor for so long.

Simplicity

The waste of processing is one of lean production's seven deadly sins.

To effectively eliminate it requires first deducing which processes are really necessary for the customer, and then attempting to reduce the number of steps in each process.

In other words, by applying the old **KISS** principle: **Keep It Simple, Stupid.**

New-age books now abound on the topic of simplifying one's life. Complexity is wearing us down.

Consider the words of the master:

"Everything should be made as simple as possible, but not simpler."

"When the solution is simple, God is answering."

"The best way is the simplest way that works."

All were spoken by the scientist considered capable of understanding the world's most complex thoughts:

Albert Einstein.

He ought to know.

ME

1. On a sheet of paper, write in large letters, the word *ME*.

2. Turn the paper upside down, then look at it in a mirror.

3. It has now changed into the word *WE*.

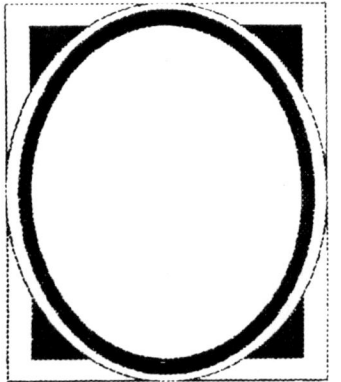

Me is in We, and We is in Me. Inside out and upside down.

Coincidence? I think not!

Chapter 5

Perfection

Who Done It?

When all is said and done, who best implements lean production will be determined by who gets the best results by setting up the best processes.

Taking a page from any good detective story, we know that to determine "who done it", we need only look to means and motive.

THE MEANS

For means, we need the *tools*, the *people*, and the *leadership*.

The *tools* are the easiest. The basics of waste elimination, kaizen, Five S, standardized work, and flow alone constitute an arsenal high powered enough to polish off almost any challenge.

The *people*? Only you will know whether or not you've got adequate human resources to handle the job. They must be flexible, creative, as well as dedicated and hard working. Most often, given adequate training, leadership, and incentives, the people arise to the occasion.

The *leadership*? They have to provide the vision as well as the tools. They have to be obsessed with supporting their workers and not with controlling them.

LEADERSHIP FOR A CHANGE

The President of DaimlerChrysler Corporation was quoted:

"Companies of the future are going to have to be able to get their employees to understand that change is constant."

In the past, lack of change ironically was considered stability which was to be admired in a corporation.

The book *Future Shock* alerted us not only to the speed of change, but to its acceleration. Stability became the dinosaur.

B.F. Skinner would argue that the best way to get your people to believe or understand something is to have them *behave* that way first.

When employees contribute kaizens on a regular basis and see their kaizens and the kaizens of their teammates become implemented, they are not only living with daily change, they are becoming an integral part of it. In fact, they become very uncomfortable if the kaizens diminish. Change becomes the norm.

Lack of change becomes the abnormal--or the defect.

Dr. Deming once commented that the reason employees fear change is that they have no control over it. Lean production, whether in the office or on the shop floor, gives employees control over their environment, control over the change.

Spare change? Never!

THE MOTIVE

The motive can be provided by leadership as part of the vision --the will to succeed, to win.

But to really be successful, we need to return to Maslow--and to people's drive to fulfill their higher order needs. Structuring work so as to allow people to fulfill these needs is how to go about it.

The key to great leadership? Not only providing the vision, tools, motivation, and support to get the job done, but also...

Providing the *spark* to individuals and teams to always do their best and to constantly strive for **perfection**. That is the path to self-actualization...

...and success for the organization.

APPENDIX

The Seven Types of Waste

Processing: Processing things that the customer doesn't want or even recognize (and is unwilling to pay for).

Waiting: Waiting for anything (people, materials, machines, or information).

Conveyance: Transporting farther than necessary or temporarily locating, restacking, or moving parts (including people, paper, and information).

Overproduction: Producing too much of something or making it too soon results in the waste of overproduction. This is the worst of the seven types of waste.

Motion: Unnecessary work movements are a form of waste. All motion or movement ideally should add value to the product or service for the customer.

Inventory: Too much of anything or anything unneeded.

Correction: Redoing, reworking, or correcting mistakes.

PRODUCTIVE PUBLICATIONS

Books to Help You Succeed

CATALOGUE

For more detailed information visit us on the Internet

Canadian Web Site:
http://www.productivepublications.ca
**or call 1-(800) 829-1317 (24 hrs) for a free
printed copy of our latest Canadian catalogue**

American Web Site:
http://www.productivepublications.com
**or call 1-(800) 850-4636 (24 hrs) for a free
printed copy of our latest American catalogue**

Serving Readers for Over 18 years

"You're Hired.... You're Fired!"

A Manager's Guide to Employee Supervision

By: Deborah L. Whitworth

This book is a great read if you are a manager or a supervisor; even if it is only being in charge temporarily for a day. It will provide you with a step-by-step method of acquiring practical human resource management skills.

Author, Deborah L. Whitworth, has been a human resource manager for over 20 years. She believes that management isn't rocket science but a process. You want to do the right thing. Unfortunately, nobody has told you what the right thing is. Deborah acts as a role model and shows you how to manage yourself, so you can be free to manager others.

144 pages, ISBN 1-55270-146-8 Softcover: Canadian: $24.95; USA $19.95; UK: £12.48

MAKE IT! MARKET IT! BANK IT!

Over 100 Ways to Start Your Own Home-Based Business

By: Barbara J. Albrecht

This book is about starting your own home-based business. It's also about earning extra money when your wages don't stretch far enough. Money for vacations and education often fall through the cracks in your financial plans and you may find that you need a second income.

Newspaper columnist, Barb Albrecht, has assembled these 100 great ideas to help you put cash into your "money jar". If you're looking to run your own part-time business or start a new career as owner of your own enterprise....you owe it to yourself to read this book.

144 pages, ISBN 1-55270-145-X softcover: Canada: $24.95 USA $19.95 UK: £12.48

Make Money Trading in Options

How to Start Immediately

By: Jason Diptee

Want to invest in an expensive stock, the Japanese Yen or the DOW but only have $200- $300 to invest? Option trading allows you to enter these markets to take advantage of investment opportunities that would otherwise require thousands of dollars. This book will teach beginners how to participate in the largely untapped and unknown area of investing that can generate profits in a matter of weeks.

Jason Diptee holds an MBA and is an experienced seminar leader on the subject of option trading.

116 pages, ISBN 1-55270-150-6 Softcover: Canadian $24.95; USA: $19.95; UK: £12.48

Welcome to the Business World:

April 2004 A Guide to Help You Get Started in Your New Job

By: V. Harvey Mortensen

You've recently graduated and you've just landed a job. Alternatively, you may have switched jobs and joined a new company. What does that really mean? What is expected of you? How will you fit in? How will you advance in the business?

V. Harvey Mortensen helps you answer these questions so that you can embark on a rewarding career in the business world. He shows you how to become a valuable "asset" for the company you work for. He also demonstrates how to plan and get organized and then to set objectives for yourself.

182 pages, ISBN 1-55270-147-6 Softcover: Canada: $26.95; USA: $21.95; UK: £13.48

You can obtain further information online at:
Canadian Web site: *http://www.productivepublications.ca*
American Web site: *http://www.productivepublications.com*
Order online or complete the order form at the end of this catalogue

**Business Planning
and Finances**

**Confederation College
Entrepreneurship Series**

**Business Relationships –
Development and
Maintenance**

**Confederation College
Entrepreneurship Series**

Business Planning and Finances takes a pragmatic and hands-on approach to business planning and financial management, and is written in straightforward language free of technical jargon. It includes a thorough review of the role of planning, the benefits to be realized from planning, and the use of a plan as a management aid.

Business Planning and Finances Confederation College Entrepreneurship Series, 174 pages, ISBN: 1-55270-091-7 Softcover   Canada: $34.95   USA: $25.95   UK: £17.48

The success of any business hinges on the effective management of three critical categories of business relationships. These are a firm's relationships with its customers, with its employees, and with the individuals and organizations that supply it with essential goods and services.

Business Relationships – Development and Maintenance Confederation College Entrepreneurship Series, 78 pages, ISBN: 1-55270-093-3, Softcover
Canada: $19.95   USA: $14.95   UK: £9.98

*Modern Materials
Management Techniques:
A Complete Guide to Help
You Plan, Direct and Control
the Purchase, Production,
Storage and Distribution of
Goods in Today's
Competitive Business
Environment–Essentials of
Supply Chain Management*

By: Paula Mackie

Covers the entire process of a company's operations relating to the acquisition of goods and services. Written for both the public and private sectors as well as college and university educators.

Modern Materials Management Techniques: 390 pages, softcover, ISBN: 1-55270-121-2   Canada: $94.95 USA: $69.95   UK: £47.48

**Software for Small
Business
2001 Edition**

**A review of the latest
Windows programs to
help you improve
business
efficiency and productivity**

By: Iain Williamson

For new and experienced users. Covers operating systems, word processing, desktop publishing, voice dictation, graphics, video, photos, spreadsheets, accounting, databases, contact management, communications, Internet software, security and virus protection.

Software for Small Business: 2001 Edition: by Iain Williamson: 345 pages, softcover; ISBN 1-55270-082-8 Canada: $39.95   USA: $29.95   UK: £19.98

**You can obtain further information online at:
Canadian Web site: *http://www.productivepublications.ca*
American Web site: *http://www.productivepublications.com*
Order online or complete the order form at the end of this catalogue**

Page 2

Web Marketing for Small & Home-Based Businesses:

How to Advertise and Sell Your Products Online

By: Learn2succeed.com Incorporated

This book shows you how to advertise and sell your products or services on the Web. Learn the basics of e-commerce and some of the challenges facing online merchants. Find out about search engines and how to improve your listings with them. Keep you name in front of your customers with permission-based e-mail and electronic newsletters. Don't forget the importance of referrals. How to use traditional marketing to drive traffic to your site. Find out about the importance of web links and associate programs.

132 pages, ISBN 1-55270-119-0 softcover: Canada: $24.95; USA: $19.95; UK: £12.48

Inexpensive E-Commerce Solutions for Small & Home-Based Businesses:

You Don't Have to Spend a Fortune to Start Selling Online

By: Learn2succeed.com Incorporated

How to sell your products or services on the Web without spending a fortune. Learn the secrets of selecting a suitable domain name. How to accept payment and how to deal with international currencies. The fulfilment process and why timely delivery is so important. Why security and privacy are such important issues for your customers and how to address them.

Take a quick tour of inexpensive e-commerce software that do not require any programming knowledge and can get you up and running in no time.

130 pages, ISBN 1-55270-118-2 softcover: Canada: $24.95; USA: $19.95 UK: £12.48

Harness the POWER of the Internet:

Easy Ways to Put Your Business on the World Wide Web

By: Michael L. Williams

Step-by-step methods to market your business, promote your wares; make a fortune....or just have a great time utilizing the Internet to its fullest advantage....this very comprehensive book shows you how to do it without any programming knowledge.

Michael L. Williams has developed and marketed educational and software programs for pre-school and grade school children. He has been Internet consultant and is now a software quality assurance engineer.

216 pages, ISBN 1-55270-142-5 Softcover Canada: $39.95; USA: $29.95; UK: £19.98

How to Get Started with Little or No Programming Knowledge

By: Michael L. Williams

This very comprehensive book covers all the essentials you need to know: domain names, web hosting, web design, Form Mail, search engines, portals and browsers. How to advertise and promote your client's business; how to fine-tune the site and find out who visits and what they look at. Learn how to become indispensable and keep your client. Find out about legal matters, tech support, maintenance fees, quality assurance, security, viruses and hackers.

Michael L. Williams has experience as a software developer and marketer, as an Internet consultant and he is now a software quality assurance engineer.

260 pages, ISBN 1-55270-143-3 Softcover: Canada: $39.95; USA: $29.95; UK: £19.98

You can obtain further information online at:
Canadian Web site: *http://www.productivepublications.ca*
American Web site: *http://www.productivepublications.com*
Order online or complete the order form at the end of this catalogue

Your Guide to Financing Business Growth by Selling a Piece of the Pie

What's involved in going public; employee share ownership plans and franchising in Canada

Revised and Updated 2003-2004 Edition

By: Iain Williamson

A critical examination of three methods of growing your business by using other people's money. How to sell shares to the public or to your employees. How to expand through franchising. The author was a financial analyst in the Canadian stockbrokerage business.

108 pages; Softcover; ISBN 1-55270-126-3; ISSN 1191-0488: Canada: $21.95

Your Guide to Canadian Export Financing: Successful Techniques for Financing Your Exports from Canada

Revised 2003-2004 Edition

By: Iain Williamson

Practical techniques for financing exports. Get details of all provincial and federal assistance programs that help you export including addresses and phone numbers to steer you in the right direction. The author is a consultant and entrepreneur who knows the practical side of importing and exporting.

Iain Williamson is an entrepreneur, business consultant and seminar leader. He has considerable experience in import-export.

174 pages; softcover; ISBN 1-55270-127-1; ISSN: 1191-047X Canada: $32.95

Your Guide to Government Financial Assistance for Business

(Separate Editions-one for each Province & Territory)

Revised 2003-2004 Editions

By: Iain Williamson

Business financing in Canada is in a constant state of flux. New government programs are continually being introduced. Old ones are often amended or discontinued with little publicity. These books will provide you with the latest information on all Federal and Provincial/Territorial programs that specifically relate to each area.

Author, Iain Williamson, of Entrepreneurial Business Consultants of Canada, has over 30 years experience as a stock market financial analyst and as owner-manager of his own companies.

Softcover: each cost $44.95
Title & ISBN List appears on right ➜

Your Guide to Government Financial Assistance for Business In...

EDITION	ISBN	PAGES
Newfoundland & Labrador	155270128X	344
Prince Edward Island	1552701298	318
Nova Scotia	1552701301	304
New Brunswick	155270131X	298
Quebec	1552701328	348
Ontario	1552701336	344
Manitoba	1552701344	354
Saskatchewan	1552701352	338
Alberta	1552701360	330
British Columbia	1552701379	344
The Yukon	1552701387	266
The Northwest Territories	1552701395	280
The Nunavut	1552701409	270

Please specify Province or Territory when ordering. All titles are $44.95 ea.

You can obtain further information online at:
Canadian Web site: *http://www.productivepublications.ca*
American Web site: *http://www.productivepublications.com*
Order online or complete the order form at the end of this catalogue

Your Guide to Starting & Self-Financing Your Own Business in Canada

Revised 2003-2004 Edition

By: Iain Williamson

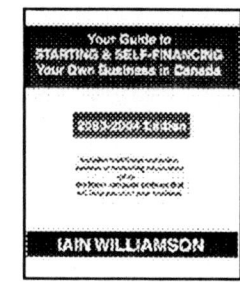

This 2003/2004 Edition has been updated and revised to reflect the many changes that have taken place in the sources of marketing information and a chapter has been added on getting marketing information from the Internet. There is a chapter on the use of computers and how they can help you run your business more efficiently and save money and time.

222 pages; Softcover; ISBN 1-55270-122-0; ISSN 1191-0518
Canada: $24.95

Your Guide to Preparing a Plan to Raise Money for Your Own Business

Revised 2003-2004 Edition

By: Iain Williamson

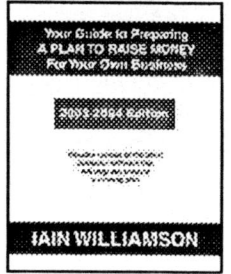

A good business plan is essential to succeed in your quest for financing. Contains a step-by-step guide to create your own winning plan. Computer software you can use. Learn how to address the concerns of investors or lenders. Tips on structuring your plan. Contains a sample plan to show you an example

The author is a consultant with many years of experience in preparing plans for business clients.

172 pages, softcover, ISBN 1-55270-123-9; ISSN 1191-0496
Canada: $24.95

Your Guide to Raising Venture Capital for Your Own Business in Canada

Revised and Updated 2003-2004 Edition

By: Iain Williamson

This book is a gold mine of information for anyone who is raising venture capital in Canada. It shows you how to do it yourself. It discusses the structure of the industry; what venture capitalists are looking for and how they evaluate deals. It tells you how to contact them. Find out what informal investors or "angels" can offer and how to find them. You can see if corporate angels and intermediaries can be of assistance.

244 pages, Softcover; ISBN 1-55270-124-7; ISSN 1191-0534   Canada: $36.95

Your Guide to Arranging Bank & Debt Financing for Your Own Business in Canada

Revised and Updated 2003-2004 Edition

By: Iain Williamson

Learn the secrets of successful debt financing in Canada. Find out who the players are in Canadian banking. Do you qualify for the new high risk, unsecured loans? How to prepare your company before you approach lenders. Find out how your loan application is evaluated. Can factoring or leasing help you? The author has many years of experience in bank financing and leasing.

230 pages; Softcover; ISBN 1-55270-125-5; ISSN 1191-0542
Canada: $32.95

You can obtain further information online at:
Canadian Web site: *http://www.productivepublications.ca*
American Web site: *http://www.productivepublications.com*
Order online or complete the order form at the end of this catalogue

Short Cut to Easy Street

How to Get Money in Your Mailbox Every Day, Plus Automatic Income for the Rest of Your Life

By: Stephen W. Kenyon

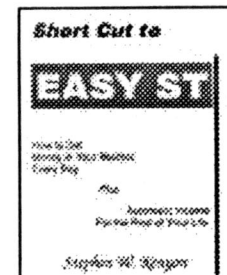

A great book on self-motivation, direct mail, self-publishing, marketing/advertising/promoting and network marketing. Study and learn the details of Stephen Kenyon's fascinating system for attracting wealth and success.

Author, **Stephen Kenyon**, shares with you the inside trade secrets and techniques which he learned over a 30-year period.

244 pages, Softcover; ISBN 1-55270-057-7 Canada: $37.95 USA: $27.95   UK: £18.98

Start Your Own Business: Be Your Own Boss!

Your Road Map to Independence

By: Iain Williamson

Learn from someone who has done it! What it takes! Where to get ideas and how to check them out. How to research the market. Calculate how much money you will really need and where to get it. Growing pains and managing employees... plus lots more.

Iain Williamson has run his own businesses for over 24 years and is a consultant. He'll help you with a Road Map to Independence!

208 pages; Softcover; ISBN 1-896210-96-1:   Canada: $29.95 USA: $21.95   UK: £14.98

Becoming Successful!

Taking Your Home-Based Business to a New Level

By: Don Varner

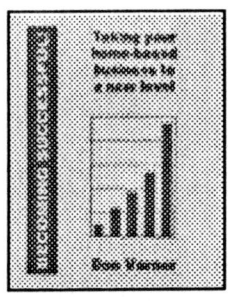

Strategies for getting great results in your home-based business! How to turn any type of business into a SUCCESSFUL business!

- Self-Improvement
- Handling Rejections
- Management Skills
- 16 Ways to Prospect
- Designing Great Ads
- Self-Motivation
- Hiring Tips
- Motivating Employees
- Closing Sales
- No-Cost Ways to Advertise

338 pgs; ISBN 1-896210-87-2; Softcover   Canada: $39.95 USA: $29.95   UK: £19.98

Timeless Strategies to Become a Successful Entrepreneur

By: Lawrence Scott Troemel

Strategies for starting, building, and managing a small business. These approaches have been successfully implemented for decades and will continue to be viable well into the future. Every entrepreneur will benefit from the advice in this very readable book that is full of interesting anecdotes.

208 pages; ISBN 1-55270-046-1; softcover: Canada: $29.95 USA: $21.95   UK: £14.98

You can obtain further information online at:
Canadian Web site: *http://www.productivepublications.ca*
American Web site: *http://www.productivepublications.com*
Order online or complete the order form at the end of this catalogue

Savvy Women Entrepreneurs

Twenty-Eight Different Women Share the Secrets To Their Business Success

By: Kristina Liehr

You don't have to go to business school to start a business! Learn how 28 remarkable women entrepreneurs started their own business; many in their garage or kitchen. Read about the steps that they took; the obstacles they overcame and the joy, happiness and success that they achieved. The chances they took and how they learned from their mistakes. Get the confidence and inspiration to start YOUR own business or EARN EXTRA INCOME.

140 pages; Softcover; ISBN 1-55270-000-3 Canada: $24.95
USA: $19.95 UK: £12.48

Can You Make Money with Your Idea or Invention?

By: Don Lunny

- Can you Exploit it?
- How to produce it
- Can you make money?
- Where to get help
- Industrial Design
- Copyright
- Points of caution
- Patent applications
- Sample licensing agreement
- Is the idea original?
- How to distribute it
- Can you protect it?
- A word about patents
- Trademarks
- First steps
- Possible problems
- What are your chances?

99 pages; softcover; ISBN 0-920847-65-X Canada: $24.95
USA: $18.95 UK: £12.48

The Canadian Business Guide to Patents for Inventions and New Products

By: George Rolston

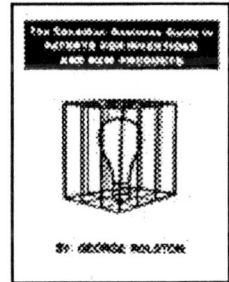

This is your complete reference to patenting around the world. The key elements in the patent process. When to search for earlier patents. When you should file patent applications. The importance of your patent filing date. Understand the critical wording of patent claims. Getting the best out of your patent agent. What the patent office will do for you. What to do if your patent application is rejected. How to go about patenting in foreign countries and how to negotiate a licence agreement. **George Rolston**, is a barrister and solicitor who has specialized in patents for over 30 years.

202 pages; ISBN 0-920847-13-7: Softcover: Canada: $48.00

Protect Your Intellectual Property

An International Guide to Patents, Copyrights and Trademarks

By: Hoyt L. Barber & Robert M. Logan

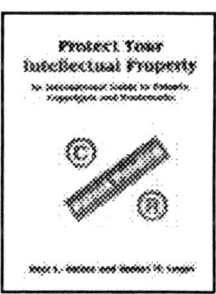

An abundance of information on step-by-step procedures to obtain exclusive protection for unique ideas, inventions, names, identifying marks, or artistic, literary, musical, photographic or cinematographic works.

Hoyt Barber is an executive with extensive experience intellectual property protection. Robert Logan is practicing U.S. attorney.

305 pages, softcover, ISBN 1-896210-95-3 Canada: $59.95
USA: $44.95 UK: £29.98

You can obtain further information online at:
Canadian Web site: *http://www.productivepublications.ca*
American Web site: *http://www.productivepublications.com*
Order online or complete the order form at the end of this catalogue

**Your Homebased
Business Plan**

-Also-

Working With Your Banker

By: Donald Lunny

**Work from Your Home
Office as an Independent
Contractor:**

**A Complete Guide
to Getting Started**

By: Chantelle Sauer

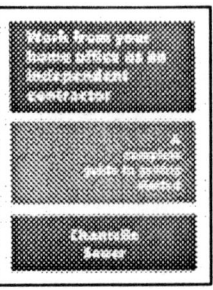

SECTION I - The Business Plan for Homebased Business:
a step-by-step guide to writing your plan.

SECTION II - Working with your Banker: the fundamentals
of borrowing and how they affect you.

Donald Lunny: an entrepreneur and consultant with many
years experience in organizing and restructuring companies.

52 pages; softcover; ISBN 0-920847-35-8   Canada: $14.95
USA: $11.95   UK: £7.48

An independent contractor is someone who works from his or
her home or home office e.g., consultants, entrepreneurs,
business owners, freelancers and outsourcers. Learn about the
advantages and disadvantages as well as the legal obligations.
Also get many ideas on how to become an independent
contractor.

Author, **Chantelle Sauer,** has spent four years as an
independent contractor. She knows from first-hand experience
how to get work.

166 pages; Softcover; ISBN 1-55270-077-1: Canada: $24.95

**How to Buy or
Sell a Business**

**Questions You Should
Ask and How to Get
the Best Price**

By: Don Lunny

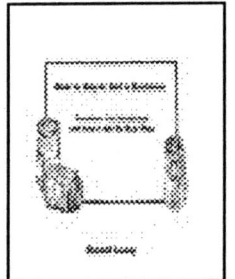

**Evaluating
Franchise Opportunities**

By: Don Lunny

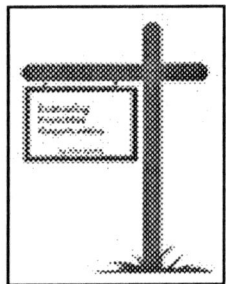

The decision to buy or sell a business requires careful
consideration. It may affect the course of the participants future
lives. Yet a surprising number of owners rush into transactions
without adequate preparation. Find out how to set the price,
locate prospects, evaluate offers, close deals and finance
purchases.

Author, **Donald Lunny,** has many years of business experience
and has been involved with the purchase and sale of many
businesses.

134 pages, ISBN 1-896210-98-8 Softcover Canada: $24.95
USA: $18.95   UK: £12.48

Although the success rate for franchisee-owned businesses is
better than for many other start-up businesses, success is not
guaranteed. Don't be "pressured" into a franchise that is not
right for you. Investigate your options. Find out how to evaluate
the business, the franchisor, the franchise package, and
yourself.

Author and business consultant, **Don Lunny,** shows you how
to avoid the pitfalls before you make a franchise investment.

75 pages; softcover; ISBN 0-920847-64-1 Canada: $19.95
USA: $14.95   UK: £9.98

**You can obtain further information online at:
Canadian Web site: *http://www.productivepublications.ca*
American Web site: *http://www.productivepublications.com*
Order online or complete the order form at the end of this catalogue**

Steps to Starting and Running a Successful Business in CANADA

By: Don Lunny

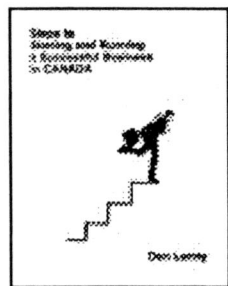

Managing your own business can be a rewarding experience but survival can be tough in today's economy. This book shows you the essential steps to ensure that your business is profitable.

Author, **Don Lunny**, is an experienced business owner and consultant with many years of experience.

190 pages; ISBN 0-920847-85-4; Softcover   Canada $34.95

Checklist for Going into Business

By: Don Lunny

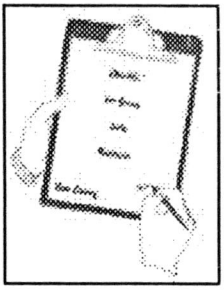

Points to create your own profitable business if this is your dream. Starting it is reality. But, there is a gap between your dream and reality - that can only be filled with careful planning. You need a plan to avoid pitfalls, to achieve your goals and make profits. This guide helps you prepare a comprehensive business plan and determine if your idea is feasible.

Don Lunny is an experienced business owner and consultant with many years of experience.

53 pages; ISBN 0-920847-86-2; softcover: Canada: $19.95
USA: $14.95   UK: £9.98

Tips for Entrepreneurs

How to meet the challenges of starting and managing your own business

By: Henry Kyambalesa

This book is the culmination of a 3-year research study into the challenges faced by entrepreneurs when they become their own boss. Tips for those about to start a business & tips for those already in business. Decide whether self-employment is for you. Practical advice on getting started. The skills you will need

Henry Kyambalesa is a tenured lecturer in Business Administration. He holsds B.B.A., M.A., and M.B.A. degrees.

194 pages softcover; ISBN 1-896210-85-6 Canada: $26.95
USA: $19.95   UK: £13.48

MAKE IT ON YOUR OWN!

How to Succeed in Your Own Business

By: Barrie Jackson

What it takes to run a business and make it succeed. Contains practical, hands-on information, for immediate use. Learn from the author's personal experience and mistakes. Lots of anecdotes from the author's business adventures which make for interesting reading with a "practical punch"

Before his untimely death, **BARRIE JACKSON**, forged Cooper Boating Centre into Canada's largest yacht charter company.

212 pgs, ISBN 1-896210-37-6; Softcover;   Canada: $29.95
USA: $21.95   UK: £14.98

You can obtain further information online at:
Canadian Web site: *http://www.productivepublications.ca*
American Web site: *http://www.productivepublications.com*
Order online or complete the order form at the end of this catalogue

**Business Planning
and Finances**

**Confederation College
Entrepreneurship Series**

**Business Relationships –
Development and
Maintenance**

**Confederation College
Entrepreneurship Series**

Business Planning and Finances takes a pragmatic and hands-on approach to business planning and financial management, and is written in straightforward language free of technical jargon. It includes a thorough review of the role of planning, the benefits to be realized from planning, and the use of a plan as a management aid.

174 pages, ISBN: 1-55270-091-7 Softcover   Canada: $34.95
USA: $25.95   UK: £17.48

The success of any business hinges on the effective management of three critical categories of business relationships. These are a firm's relationships with its customers, with its employees, and with the individuals and organizations that supply it with essential goods and services.

78 pages, ISBN: 1-55270-093-3, Softcover   Canada: $19.95
USA: $14.95   UK: £9.98

**How to Write a Million Dollar
Adventure Novel**

**Novel Writing as a
Profitable Profession**

By: Dr. Ray Mesluk

**Software for Small
Business
2001 Edition**

**A review of the latest
Windows programs to
help you improve
business
efficiency and productivity**

By: Iain Williamson

A structured approach to writing your novel quickly and easily. Master the techniques of novel writing and turn them into a profitable career.

304 pages, ISBN 1-55270-001-1 softcover Canada: $34.95
USA: $25.95   UK: £17.48

For new and experienced users. Covers operating systems, word processing, desktop publishing, voice dictation, graphics, video, photos, spreadsheets, accounting, databases, contact management, communications, Internet software, security and virus protection.

345 pages, softcover; ISBN 1-55270-082-8   Canada: $39.95
USA: $29.95   UK: £19.98

**You can obtain further information online at:
Canadian Web site: *http://www.productivepublications.ca*
American Web site: *http://www.productivepublications.com*
Order online or complete the order form at the end of this catalogue**

Entrepreneurship and Starting a Business

Confederation College Entrepreneurship Series

Entrepreneurship and Starting a Business provides a comprehensive introduction to entrepreneurs and what they do, and is a must-read for anyone who has aspirations to start and run their own business. The book examines entrepreneurs, their values and behaviour, and factors that contribute to their success and failure. It also takes an in-depth look at how they spot business opportunities or come up with business ideas.

110 pages, ISBN: 1-55270-090-9 Softcover   Canada: $24.95
USA: $18.95   UK: £12.48

Small Business Finance

Confederation College Entrepreneurship Series

Small Business Finance was designed with the start-up business owner/manager in mind and provides a detailed overview of the organization and operation of a business from a financial perspective. Developed as a combination textbook and workbook, it takes the reader step-by-step through each element of a company's finances from pre-startup costs all the way to record keeping and financial monitoring for an established business.

136 pages, ISBN: 1-55270-092-5 Softcover   Canada: $29.95
USA: $21.95   UK: £14.98

Youth Entrepreneurship

Confederation College Entrepreneurship Series

Some of North America's most successful businesses have been started by people between the ages of 15 and 25. If you are a young person with a business idea or a desire to start your own business then this informative and practical book should be a must-read for you. Learn from the experiences of others and improve your prospects for success.

108 pages, ISBN: 1-55270-094-1 Softcover   Canada: $24.95
USA: $18.95   UK: £12.48

The Entrepreneur and the Business Idea

Confederation College Entrepreneurship Series

If you ever wondered what entrepreneurs are like; where they look for business ideas and opportunities, and what kinds of thinking and tools some of them use in their approach to a possible business start-up, then this introductory book should prove very helpful to you. It includes both a self-assessment and a business opportunity assessment tool, and advocates a "damage control approach" to getting into business.

50 pages, ISBN: 1-55270-089-5 Softcover   Canada: $14.95
USA: $10.95   UK: £7.48

You can obtain further information online at:
Canadian Web site: *http://www.productivepublications.ca*
American Web site: *http://www.productivepublications.com*
Order online or complete the order form at the end of this catalogue

Anybody Can Sell!

**Sales Strategies to
Increase Your
Business Profits**

By: Don Varner

**The Basics for
Sales Success**

**An Essential Guide for New
Sales Representatives,
Entrepreneurs and
Business People**

By: Bill Sobye

Written for those who have started a business and have limited selling experience.

- Covers creative marketing and sales presentations.
- Hints on self-motivation and how to handle rejection.
- Discusses different kinds of buyers and how to handle them.

102 pages; ISBN 1-55270-004-6; Softcover Canada: $18.95
USA: $14.95   UK: £9.48

An introductory book which covers the basic points on how to:

- Find customers
- Dress for success
- Set goals
- Success and rejection
- Study your prospects
- Handle "the butterflies"
- How to include humour
- Business versus pleasure

Bill Sobye has 28 years of experience as a Sales Manager.

157 pages; Softcover; ISBN 1-896210-65-1   Canada: $24.95
USA: $18.95   UK: £12.48

MEETING THE SAMURAI

**Two Hundred Power
Strategies for Doing
Business in Japan**

By: Jonathan King

**Reach the Global
Marketplace**

**A Canadian Guide
to Researching
Foreign Markets
and Online Sources**

By: Richard B. McEachin

Author, **Jonathan King**, learned the language and worked in Japan for six years as a business consultant and director to two Japanese "Fortune 500" companies. In this book he shows you how to export your products to the heart of Asia's largest, yet toughest economic market.

119 pages, softcover, ISBN 1-896210-40-6   Canada: $19.95
USA: $14.95   UK: £9.98

Advice on hiring an outside researcher. Shows you what is available online and in print. Written for both the newcomer and the experienced exporter. Author, **Richard B. McEachin**, is an expert with over 20 years experience in gathering and analyzing intelligence material.

193 pages; ISBN 0-920847-92-7; softcover Canada: $24.95

**You can obtain further information online at:
Canadian Web site: *http://www.productivepublications.ca*
American Web site: *http://www.productivepublications.com*
Order online or complete the order form at the end of this catalogue**

Marketing for Beginners

How to Get Your Products into the Hands of Consumers

By: Iain Williamson

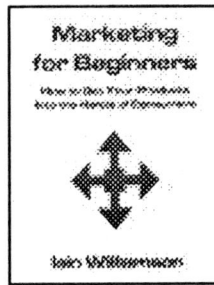

Marketing Beyond 2000

Why you will have to use the Internet to market your goods or services in the 21st. Century

By: Iain Williamson

Covers the basics of marketing for new entrepreneurs. How to make people aware of your products. How to get them to buy. How to get products into the hands of consumers. Traditional channels of distribution versus direct marketing. One-on-one marketing versus mass marketing. A look at the Internet as a marketing tool. Ways to promote and advertise your products. After-sales service and the lifetime value of your customers. Sources of marketing information. The author has been marketing products for 20 years.

215 pages, Softcover, ISBN 1-896210-97-X   Canada: $29.95 USA: $21.95   UK: £14.98

The Internet will become an awesome marketing tool in the 21st. Century. Learn how its current limitations are being overcome. Take a look at the future of radio, TV and newspapers. Glimpse at the marketplace of the future. The author says it's up to you to take advantage of this tremendous marketing tool. Find out how!

194 pages, ISBN 1-896210-66-X; softcover Canada: $27.95 USA: 21.95   UK: £13.98

Selling by Mail Order and Independence

By: Donald Lunny

Successful Direct Mail Marketing in Canada

A Step-by-Step Guide to Selling Your Products or Services Through the Mail

By: Iain Williamson

Your step-by-step guide to seeking independence with your own mail order business. Also invaluable, if you are an established business owner who wants to add a mail order department or to purchase an existing mail order business. Learn the essentials from

Donald Lunny, who is a business consultant with over 25 years experience in sales, marketing and promotion in Canada.

109 pages; Softcover; ISBN 0-920847-24-2   Canada: $16.95 USA: 12.95   UK: £8.48

Techniques to Make Money in the Highly Competitive Direct Mail Market. Direct mail as an inexpensive way to reach customers. Ways to keep your costs to a minimum. How to save on postage by using bulk rates. How to get the most out of your computer.

The author has over 15 years experience selling by direct mail.

114 pages, softcover; ISBN 1-896210-39-2; Canada: $19.95

You can obtain further information online at:
Canadian Web site: *http://www.productivepublications.ca*
American Web site: *http://www.productivepublications com*
Order online or complete the order form at the end of this catalogue

**Secrets of Successful
Advertising and Promotion**

**Practical Steps to Growing
Your Business**

By: Don Varner

- Covers all the basics of advertising and promoting for business.
- How to prospect for more customers.
- How to increase the average size of your sales.

Author, **Don Varner**, is an expert with many years of experience in this area.

158 pages; Softcover; ISBN 1-55270-002-X Canada: $24.95
USA: $18.95   UK: £12.48

**How to Deliver Excellent
Customer Service**

**A Step-by-Step Guide
for Every Business**

By: Julie Olley

A pre-designed workbook approach for businesses that wish to develop, impler analyse and follow-up customer service projects. Step-by "HOW TO:" ideas and sample formats are included suggestions can be implemented over time.

Author, **Julie Olley**, was formerly National Manager of Qu Assurance with a major international travel organization. has designed several curricula for The Canadian Scho Management and International Business.

160 pages, Softcover; ISBN 1-55270-045-3 Canada: $2
USA: $19.95   UK: £13.48

**Jump Start Your
New Employees**

**Get the Most Out of
New Hires From Their
First Day on the Job!**

By: Julie Olley

An organizational tool for various employee transitions with suggested steps to boost initial productivity of new employees from their first day on the job; to minimize the impact on your customers and identify training needs. Also, to professionally handle departing employees while maintaining security and company property. How employee transitions can be used to create a positive impact on your customers.

64 pages, softcover; ISBN 1-55270-084-4 Canada: $12.95
USA: $9.95   UK: £6.48

**The Canadian Business
Owners Guide to
Salary Administration**

**Entrepreneurial Business
Consultants of Canada**

Salary Administration Program provides the means management to:

- Properly analyse and evaluate positions.
- Provide equitable and competitive remuneration.
- Appraise individual performance in the position.

164 pages; ISBN 0-920847-11-0; softcover Canada: $39.

**You can obtain further information online at:
Canadian Web site: *http://www.productivepublications.ca*
American Web site: *http://www.productivepublications.com*
Order online or complete the order form at the end of this catalogue**

An Introduction to Personal Computers

What You Need to Know to Get Up and Running

By: Stephen Belaire

This book will get you from where you are now in computer knowledge, to where you absolutely should be, in the straightest line possible. It will not take a major commitment of your time to get through this book.

Stephen Belaire, has held different positions in the Information Systems field and lives and breathes computers. He is a college instructor who teaches people how to use them.

140 pages., Softcover; ISBN 1-55270-078-X Canada: $29.95 USA: $21.95   UK: £14.98

Welcome to the Fun World of Computers–Become a "Geek" in No Time! Neat Things You Can Do When You Buy a Computer

by Thomas P. Bun

When the uninitiated bystander encounters the personal computer for the first time, a primordial fear often arises. "This looks really complicated. I may need a Ph.D. before I can take a first step with this." Nothing could be farther from the truth. These pages show that you can start with great ease, and in a short time a large number of useful activities may be carried out with its aid, while spending time in a most agreeable and enjoyable way.

80 pages, ISBN: 1-55270-120-4 Softcover   Canada: $19.95 USA: $14.95   UK: £9.98

THE ONLINE WORLD

How to Profit from the Information Superhighway

By: Mike Weaver and Odd de Presno

This book will change the way you learn, find a job, get information & do business. By the year 2000, the Internet will have one billion users. Can you afford to ignore this market?

Odd de Presno, from Norway, is a consultant and **Mike Weaver**, from Saskatchewan, is winner of the Saskatchewan Association for Computers in Education/Apple Teacher Award of Excellence.

302 pages, softcover; ISBN 0-920847-89-7   Canada: $39.95 USA: $29.95   UK: £19.98

THE NET EFFECT

Will the Internet be a Panacea or Curse for Business and Society in the Next Ten Years?

By: Iain Williamson

Are you ready for the greatest change to business & society since the Industrial Revolution? Examine the world ten years from now when entire sectors of the economy may be eliminated and others will be born. Find out who will be the winners and losers and how it will affect you. Prepare for the dramatic changes that are coming!

244 pages, softcover, ISBN 1-896210-38-4;   Canada: $29.95

You can obtain further information online at:
Canadian Web site: *http://www.productivepublications.ca*
American Web site: *http://www.productivepublications.com*
Order online or complete the order form at the end of this catalogue

**Accounting Software
for Small Business**

**A Complete Review Based
on the Results of a Survey
by 1850 Accounting
Professionals Who
Evaluated 1000 Key Features
(Year 2000/2001 -
Canadian Edition)**

Targeted at the over 900,000 small and home businesses in Canada to assist in the selection of the most appropriate software. The survey is divided into three sections. The first rates ten factors: stability, performance, flexibility. ease of use, feature set, reporting, integration with Microsoft Office, e-commerce, third party software and technical support. The second section rates the software by module and the third section contains general comments. Edited by **Alan Salmon**, seminar leader and expert in accounting software.

322 pages, ISBN 1-55270-052-6; softcover; Year 2000/2001 - Canadian Edition Canada: $134.95

**Install Your Own
E-Commerce Server for
Your Home Or Business**

**An Inexpensive Way to
Start Your Own
Online Business With
Easy Step-by-Step
Instructions on How to
Get Up and Running**

By: Don Artman

Based on Microsoft® NT Server 4.0 and a cable modem, this book shows you how to start your own inexpensive e-commerce site. If you already own a Pentium® computer, Don Artman will show you how to do it for under $1,000 (US).

Just as Henry Ford brought the inexpensive automobile to the people, **Don Artman** brings you an affordable e-commerce solution. His book is full of straightforward, step-by-step instructions on how to do it.

248 pages; Softcover; ISBN 1-55270-083-6: Canada: $39.95
USA: $29.05 UK: £19.98

**Are You Ready for
Information Warfare?**

**Security for Personal
Computers, Networks
and Telecommunication
Systems**

Gregory J. Petrakis, Ph.D.

This book is an antidote against hackers and information theft. Access to data is so easy to obtain and it can be stolen or modified. Informational infrastructures can also be destroyed. This book shows you how to counter-attack. The author is an Adjunct Professor at the University of Missouri-Kansas City.

206 pages, softcover; ISBN 1-896210-94-5; Canada: $34.95
USA: $26.95 UK: £17.48

**Learn UNIX in
Fifteen Days**

**by: Dwight Baer and
Paul Davidson**

This book was written out of the need for a text which presented the material which was actually taught and tested in a typical UNIX course at the college level. It is not intended to replace a comprehensive UNIX manual, but for most students who have not yet spent five years learning all the "eccentricities" of the UNIX Operating System, it will present all they need to know (and more!) in order to use and support a UNIX system.

176 pages, ISBN: 1-55270-087-9 Softcover   Canada: $34.95
USA: $26.95 UK: £17.48

**You can obtain further information online at:
Canadian Web site: *http://www.productivepublications.ca*
American Web site: *http://www.productivepublications.com*
Order online or complete the order form at the end of this catalogue**

Critical Analysis in Decision-Making:

Conventional and "Outside the Box" Approaches to Developing Solutions to Today's Business Challenges

by: James Briggs

This book examines why some people to make good business decisions more effectively, more often, than others. Great leaders in the public service, business, and the non-profit sectors, remind us that an effective decision-making process is the key to solving problems for any organization. Effective organizations search for leaders who have good problem solving skills.

234 pages, ISBN: 1-55270-116-6 Softcover   Canada:$39.95
USA: $29.95   UK: £19.98

THE LEAN OFFICE

How to Use Just-in-Time Techniques to Streamline Your Office

By: Jim Thompson

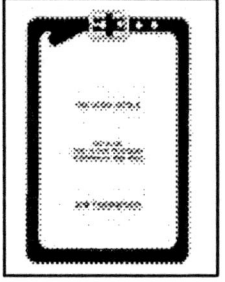

This book is for everyone who works in an office. Find out how to foster and nurture employee involvement and put excitement back into continuous improvement. Get the tools needed to improve office productivity. Most importantly, reduce employee stress and frustration, while improving productivity. Find out how this happens with employees, not to employees!

Jim Thompson is a lean production consultant who studied these systems first-hand while with GM and Toyota in California.

138 pages, softcover, ISBN 1-896210-41-4 Canada: $24.95
USA: $19.95 UK:£12.48

LEAN PRODUCTION

How to Use the Highly Effective Japanese Concept of Kaizen to Improve Your Efficiency

By: Jim Thompson

Learn specific techniques and behaviours to improve your effectiveness. Find out about a system that has been used very effectively at the organizational level for over forty years.

Author, **Jim Thompson** has held senior management positions with General Motors and the Walker Manufacturing Company.

146 pages, softcover, ISBN 1-896210-42-2; Canada: $24.95
USA: $19.95   UK: £12.48

LEAN PRODUCTION FOR THE OFFICE

Common Sense Ideas To Help Your Office Continuously Improve

By: Jim Thompson

More ideas for everyone who works in an office:

Be idea-driven	Reduce frustration
Add value	Let others benchmark you

How to use employees' creativity and ingenuity. Employees' feelings **do** count. Author, **Jim Thompson**, is the guru of applying lean production to the office environment.

136 pages, softcover, ISBN 1-55270-025-9 Canada: $24.95
USA: $19.95   UK: £12.48

You can obtain further information online at:
Canadian Web site: *http://www.productivepublications.ca*
American Web site: *http://www.productivepublications.com*
Order online or complete the order form at the end of this catalogue

Project Management:
Welcome Opportunity
or Awesome Burden?

by: Robert G. Edwards

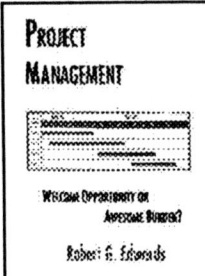

Effective Management:

Interpersonal Skills that
Will Help You Earn
the Respect and
Commitment of Employees

By: Dave Day Ph.D.

This concise, how-to, self-help guide will help both aspiring and practicing project managers. Its content was developed during the author's forty-four years in professional engineering and project management. The principles and practices that he describes are based on his personal experience and can easily be applied to most simple or complex projects.

170 pages, ISBN: 1-55270-086-0 Soft.cover, Canada: $26.95 USA: $20.95 UK: £13.48

Ten key interpersonal skills for the manager... from choosing a leadership style to the day of completing annual performance evaluations. Contains practical suggestions to increase the productivity and commitment of all employees. Essential reading for all new managers and a resource for existing managers.

Dave Day has over 35 years experience as a manager, consultant and Professor of Management at Columbia College.

182 pages, ISBN 1-896210-99-6; Softcover Canada: $27.95 USA: $21.95 UK: £13.98

Cooperative Time
Management
Get more done and
have more fun!

Chance Massaro &
Katheryn Allen-Katz

Leadership with Panache

52 Ways to Set Yourself
Apart as a
Dynamic Manager

By: Jeff Jernigan

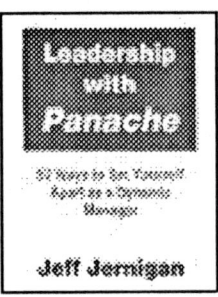

Cntains the wisdom of the last fifty years of research and writing about time management together with my eighteen years working in organizations helping people get the most satisfying results. It is intended for people who want to have goals and want to achieve them. It is interactive and easy to use.The authors are time management experts. Follow the steps which they outline in this 226 page workbook and YOUR RESULTS WILL BE REMARKABLE!

224 pages, softcover; ISBN 1-896210-86-4; Canada: $34.95 USA: $25.95 UK: £17.48

This book cuts to the underbelly of leadership in the modern organization. Divided into 52 "Ways" so that you can select one topic each week of the year for group discussion with your management and supervisory associates. Poses hard hitting questions for consideration.

Author, **Jeff Jernigan,** has over 25-years experience as an organizational development specialist providing companies support in creating, continuing and capitalizing on change. He is the recipient of numerous industry awards.

180 pages Softcover ISBN 1-55270-081-X Canada: $29.95 USA: $21.95 UK: £12.48

You can obtain further information online at:
Canadian Web site: *http://www.productivepublications.ca*
American Web site: *http://www.productivepublications.com*
Order online or complete the order form at the end of this catalogue

Market Overseas with Canadian Government Help

By: Don Lunny

Finding Overseas Buyers
Meeting New Customers
Displaying Products Abroad
Conducting Market Research
Government Assistance
Export and Import Permits
Reading to Find Markets
Other helpful sources

Export Questionnaire
Distributors Questionnaire
Export Costing/Pricing
Goods and Services Tax
Thinking in Global Terms
Start with North America
The Bank and the Exporter
Private Sector Financing

68 p ISBN 0-920847-87-0 softcover Canada: $19.95

Everything I Know About Marketing I Learned from High Priced Call Girls

A Marketing Manual for Everyone Who Sells Themselves for A Living

By: Jerome Shore

This book can be instrumental in the success of people who sell personal services. The audience includes lawyers, accountants, consultants, wellness therapistss and others. The marketing skills that make call girls successful are the same as those needed by anyone who sells experience and know-how.

Author, **Jerome Shore**, has been involved with advertising for over twenty years and holds an MBA.

202 pages; Softcover; ISBN 1-55270-054-2
Canada: $27.95   USA: $21.95   UK: £13.98

Speak with Confidence NOW!

A Simple, Unique Program Designed to Make You a Confident, Effective, Dynamic Speaker Every Day, in Every Situation!

By Steve Ryan

Surveys show that speaking in public is our greatest fear. Top-rated radio host and training expert, Steve Ryan, shows you how to make presentations using dynamic speech. Conquer nervousness, improve your breathing habits and enunciation. Learn to avoid vocal mistakes. How to project yourself and use vocabulary and body language advantageously.

Author, **Steve Ryan** hosts the top-rated *KILO/Colorado Springs Morning Show*. He has been in radio for over 16 years.

168 pages Softcover;   ISBN : 1-896210-62-7 Canada: $24.95
USA: $18.95   UK: £12.48

Enthusiasm Pays!

How to Use it Effectively in Your Business

By: Don Varner

People love enthusiasm!

Learn how to use it effectively in your business:

▸ How to evoke favourable responses.
▸ Enthusiasm is a high paid quality.
▸ Five steps to your success.

54 pages, ISBN 1-55270-003-8; Softcover Canada: $14.95
USA: $11.95   UK: £7.48

You can obtain further information online at:
Canadian Web site: *http://www.productivepublications.ca*
American Web site: *http://www.productivepublications.com*
Order online or complete the order form at the end of this catalogue

Money Management

A First Course

By: H.J. Fluke

A textbook that demystifies the wealth building process and guides young readers through a wide range of business topics while teaching the principles of personal financial management. Part I covers economics; Part II covers economics from the business viewpoint; Part III covers personal financial planning; Part IV deals with entering the workforce and Part V covers economic activity between nations. Written by **H.J. Fluke**, a business teacher.

136 pages; Softcover; ISBN 1-55270-079-8   Canada: $29.95 US: $21.95   UK: £14.98

Let's be Reasonable!

Effective ways to handle difficult people

By: Clive Lilwall

This book will help you deal with the difficult people in your business and personal lives. It discusses numerous reasons for nastiness and offers you many practical solutions.

Clive Lilwall has taught human communications and writing at Durham College for 28 years and shows you effective ways to handle the difficult people in your life.

172 pages; Softcover; ISBN 1-896210-64-3   Canada: $29.95   USA: $21.95   UK: £14.98

The Ontario Business Owners Guide on How to Meet the Challenge of Pay Equity

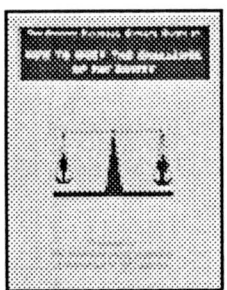

Provides you with a step-by-step guide on how to implement a salary administration scheme that will satisfy the requirements of the Ontario Act. It shows you how to prepare a pay equity plan.

260 pgs; ISBN 0920847-12-9; softcover; price: Canada: $49.95

Market Overseas with Canadian Government Help

By: Don Lunny

Finding Overseas Buyers
Meeting New Customers
Displaying Products Abroad
Conducting Market Research
Government Assistance
Export and Import Permits
Reading to Find Markets
Other helpful sources

Export Questionnaire
Distributors Questionnaire
Export Costing/Pricing
Goods and Services Tax
Thinking in Global Terms
Start with North America
The Bank and the Exporter
Private Sector Financing

68 pages ISBN 0-920847-87-0 softcover Canada: $19.95

You can obtain further information online at:
Canadian Web site: *http://www.productivepublications.ca*
American Web site: *http://www.productivepublications.com*
Order online or complete the order form at the end of this catalogue

The Internet Job Search Guide

By Cathy & Dan Noble

A thorough and comprehensive guide to finding employment opportunities using the Internet. You will learn about resume assistance; career guidance; research and networking. This book takes a step-by-step approach. Contains hundreds of Internet addresses covering a wide spectrum of employment opportunities. This guide will help both first-time users as well as experienced net surfers. It is concise and easy to read.

208 pages; Softcover; ISBN 1-896210-63-5   Canada: $29.95
USA: $21.95   UK: £14.98

HOW TO SELL YOURSELF INTO A JOB

Successful Job Hunting Using Sales and Marketing Know-How

By: Dr. Ray Mesluk

Worried about the difficult questions you might be asked in an interview? Are you focussed on your lack of experience? Do you like to talk about your accomplishments & qualifications? Stop thinking "my failings", "my successes", "me".

Learn from **Dr. Ray Mesluk**, an expert with a Ph.D. in Mathematics who has applied sales and marketing techniques in his job searches. He has worked for a leading recruitment firm.

184 pages; ISBN 0-920847-91-9; softcover Canada: $29.95
USA: $21.95   UK: £14.98

HOW TO GET A JOB!

By: Paul Shearstone

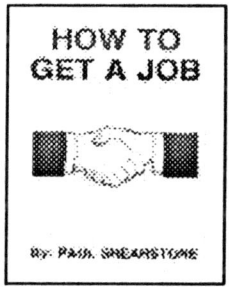

Learn interview fundamentals How to prepare mentally
What makes a good résumé   Types of interviewers
Ways to maintain credibility Reason for different questions
Master the confident answer How to turn the tables
How to ask for the job   How to GET THE JOB!

Paul Shearstone is President of Colby Lewis Management Consultants and an experienced recruiter and sales trainer.

Softcover:

English Edition: 54 pages; ISBN 0-920847-36-6
Canada: $14.95 USA: $11.95 UK: £7.48

French\English Bilingual Edition: ISBN 0-920847-37-4
Canada: $24.95 USA: $18.95 £12.48

---

30 Minutes to a Better Job!

Step-by-Step Instructions for Getting a Better Job Made Easy!

By Don Varner

Applies to any age, any educational level & in any field!
Get a job that makes you happy!

Earn more money!   Create killer résumés!
Free job counseling!   Secrets of interviewing!
Make them want you!   How to land that great job!
Locate over 33,000 jobs & their salaries!
"The only job security in today's society is knowing where the next job is and how to get it!"

52 pages; ISBN 1-896210-89-9 softcover   Canada: $9.95
USA: $7.99 UK:£4.98

You can obtain further information online at:
Canadian Web site: *http://www.productivepublications.ca*
American Web site: *http://www.productivepublications.com*
Order online or complete the order form at the end of this catalogue

**SUCCESS is the
Best Revenge:
Gold Medal
Career Management**

**By: John Stewardson
and Bob Evans**

**How to Get a
Really Great Job!**

**A Complete Program
if You Hate Your Job
and Don't Know
How to Go About
Changing It**

By Donald L Varner

- A timely book for "The Brave New World" of job searches
- Practical advice to show you how to win at the career game
- Read it if you are employed or are looking for a job

John Stewardson and **Bob Evans,** between them have fifty years experience in human resources, contract operating executives and executive outplacement and career planning.

277 pages, softcover, ISBN 0-920847-88-9;   Canada: $39.95 USA: $29.29   UK: £19.98

This book is written for people at any age; at any educational level;for any field; in any market! If you follow Don Varner's advice, you can watch your happiness and your salary soar... as your job turns into a career!

240 pages; Softcover; ISBN 1-896210-90-2 Canada: $29.95 USA: $21.95   UK: £14.98

**A Guerrilla Manual for
the Adult College Student**

**How to Go to College
(Almost) Full Time in
Your Spare Time... and
Still Have Time to Hold
Down a Job, Raise a
Family, Pay the Bills,
and Have Some Fun!**

By: Mike Doolin

Biological Happiness

**Nature's Secrets for
Successful Living**

By: Claude Maranda, M.D.

This is a "how to" book. It's intentionally short on theory, long on practice. It's full of the mistakes the author and others made and provides advice on how to avoid making them yourself.

Author, **Mike Doolin,** has been there. He will help you develop the personal organization you absolutely must have to get a college education while your life is full of a lot of other responsibilities.

296 pages; Softcover; ISBN 1-55270-048-8   Canada: $34.95 USA: $26.95   UK: £17.48

Happiness is the most significant preoccupation of mankind. This book lets you examine the medical, biological, anthropological and philosophical underpinnings of happiness. The author unmasks religious wishful thinking, spiritual "mumbo-jumbo", and the traditional psycho-babble found in print.

Dr. Maranda is Physician-in-Chief at a Montreal hospital. Learn from him how to increase YOUR state of Happiness.

404 pages; Softcover; ISBN 1-55270-024-0   Canada: $48.95 USA: $36.95   UK: £24.48

**You can obtain further information online at:
Canadian Web site:** *http://www.productivepublications.ca*
American Web site: *http://www.productivepublications.com*
Order online or complete the order form at the end of this catalogue

Salary Administration

Prepared by:
Entrepreneurial Business
Consultants of Canada

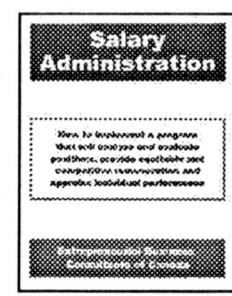

Take Control
of Your Money

Success Starts With the
Opportunity to Plan for
the Rest of Your Life

(American Edition)

By: Donald J. Davison

Salary Administration Program provides the means for management to:

- Properly analyse and evaluate positions.
- Provide equitable and competitive remuneration.
- Appraise individual performance in the position.

Salary Administration prepared by Entrepreneurial Business Consultants of Canada; 164 pages; ISBN 1-55270-085-2; Softcover;   Canada: $39.95   USA: $29.95   UK: £19.98

You have needs and wants. But the way in which you manage your time and money depends on your stage in life (single, married, divorced, working, retired, etc.) together with your value system. It is up to you to take a long look at yourself and decide if you want to control your lifestyle or not. If you do ... then read this book.

Author, **Donald J. Davison**, was a banker who went through a divorce and an earlier-than-planned retirement. These experiences taught him a lot about being a single parent, a senior and a survivor.

Take Control of Your Money by Donald J. Davison: 260 pages; Softcover; ISBN 1-55270-080-1   USA: $29.95

The Old Mission Academy

A Novel of One Charter
School's Experiences
Implementing
Lean Education

By: J. K. Thompson

A novel about more learning for less money. It suggests that it is possible to remove the waste from education using lean production business concepts. It also outlines the controversial issues surrounding the establishment of charter schools. The book ties this into the basics of lean production, which is changing the very nature of how the world will be making things in the 21st century.

The Old Mission Academy by J.K. Thompson, 206 pages; ISBN 1-896210-91-0; Softcover   USA: $21.95

VISIT OUR WEB SITES FOR THE LATEST
ON BOOKS TO HELP YOU SUCCEED

Canada:
http://www.prouctivepublications.com

USA:
http://www.prouctivepublications.com

You can obtain further information online at:
Canadian Web site: *http://www.productivepublications.ca*
American Web site: *http://www.productivepublications.com*
Order online or complete the order form at the end of this catalogue

Salary Administration

Prepared by:
Entrepreneurial Business
Consultants of Canada

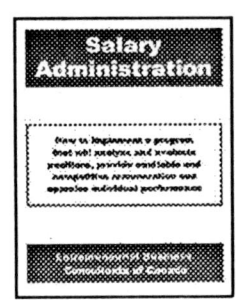

Salary Administration Program provides the means for management to:

- Properly analyse and evaluate positions.
- Provide equitable and competitive remuneration.
- Appraise individual performance in the position.

164 pages; ISBN 1-55270-085-2; Softcover;   Canada: $39.95
USA: $29.95   UK: £19.98

Take Control
of Your Money

Success Starts With the
Opportunity to Plan for
the Rest of Your Life

(American Edition)

By: Donald J. Davison

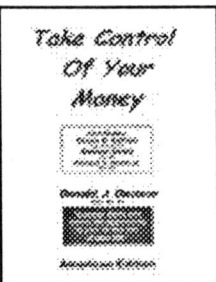

You have needs and wants. But the way in which you manage your time and money depends on your stage in life (single, married, divorced, working, retired, etc.) together with your value system. It is up to you to take a long look at yourself and decide if you want to control your lifestyle or not. If you do ... then read this book.

Author, **Donald J. Davison**, was a banker who went through a divorce and an earlier-than-planned retirement. These experiences taught him a lot about being a single parent, a senior and a survivor.

260 pages; Softcover; ISBN 1-55270-080-1 USA: $29.95

The Old Mission Academy

A Novel of One Charter
School's Experiences
Implementing
Lean Education

By: J. K. Thompson

A novel about more learning for less money. It suggests that it is possible to remove the waste from education using lean production business concepts. It also outlines the controversial issues surrounding the establishment of charter schools. The book ties this into the basics of lean production, which is changing the very nature of how the world will be making things in the 21st century.

206 pages; ISBN 1-896210-91-0; Softcover   USA: $21.95

She Delivers Steel

Inspiration from a
Grandmother who
Drove Her Dream
to Reality

By: Patricia Prior

Fulfill your dreams - accomplish your goals both physical and emotional! At age 43, **Patricia Prior** left a successful career in motivational speaking to fulfill her dream of becoming a truck driver. She hauled steel through the Rockies to Vancouver and seven years later she became a grandmother! Her story reflects the true concept of real accomplishment. The journey is rewarding. Read this book and enjoy the trip!

162 pages, softcover; ISBN 1-896210-92-9; Canada: $24.95
USA: $18.95   UK: £12.48

You can obtain further information online at:
Canadian Web site: *http://www.productivepublications.ca*
American Web site: *http://www.productivepublications.com*
Order online or complete the order form at the end of this catalogue

TAX HAVENS FOR CANADIANS

Ingenious Ways to Preserve Your Wealth (and Have Fun Doing It!)

By: Adam Starchild

Are you overtaxed? The offshore solution is your answer. Details on 37 tax havens & what they offer. Tax havens are now within reach of Canada's "middle class". Learn how to save as much as half of your annual taxes. Protect your assets from professional malpractice suits, divorce proceedings, or no-fault liability suits. **Adam Starchild** is the author of many dozen books and articles.

341 pages, softcover; ISBN 1-896210-18-X; Canada: $48.95

Slot Machines: Fun Machines or Tax Machines?

A Technician Reveals the Truth About One-Armed Bandits

By: Ian B. Williams

How slot machines work and how to play them. Covers the pay-out systems. Will help you have a better casino experience. Also examines the social implications of slot machines in our society; both the positive and negative.

Ian B. Williams is a certified electronics technician and a trained slot technician, who worked for several years in the casino industry

134 pages; Softcover; ISBN 1-55270-049-6   Canada: $24.95
USA: 19.95   UK: £12.48

STOCK MARKET PANIC!

How to Prosper in the Coming Crash

Dave Skarica

A warning for every mutual fund and stock investor! The sharp sell-off in late August 1998 showed how confidence can erode overnight. How do you avoid watching your wealth evaporate? Find out How to Prosper in the Coming Crash!

228 pages, softcover; ISBN 1-896210-93-7   Canada: $29.95
USA: $24.95   UK: £12.48

Shoplifting, Security, Curtailing Crime - Inside & Out

By: Don Lunny

If you are a shopkeeper or business owner, this practical, hands-on book will alert you to the alarming theft rates you may be exposed to. From petty theft, bad cheques to armed robbery, you get advice on dealing with the situation and how to train staff.

Discusses internal theft by employees - how you can recognize it and how to reduce it. If it alerts you to just one problem, it could pay for itself many, many times over.

115 pages; softcover; ISBN 0-920847-66-8:   Canada: $29.95
USA: $21.95   UK: £14.98

ORDER FORM

Qty.	Title	Price
	ADD Postage: $7.00 first title for USA & Canada UK:£11.20	
	ADD $1.25 Postage per title thereafter USA/Can UK: £1.80	
	SUB-TOTAL	
	ADD 7% GST - Canadian Residents Only (others EXEMPT)	
	TOTAL	

Name_____

Organization_____

Street_____

City/Town_____State/Prov_____ Zip/Postal Code_____

Phone_____Fax_____

☐ Cheque   ☐ VISA   ☐ MasterCard   ☐ American Express
Credit Card Orders: can be faxed to: + (416) 322-7434

Card
Number_____

Expiry Date (Month/Year)_____

Cardholder Signature_____

Mail to: **Productive Publications**
PO Box 7200, Stn. A, Toronto, Ontario M5W 1X8
Phone: (416) 483-0634 Fax: (416) 322-7434

Page 26